Rejoicing the heart

The Psalms Illustrated

Esther Walker

RIVERSTONE
GROUP
PUBLISHING

ISBN 978-0-9906166-9-6

Published by: Riverstone Group, LLC, Jasper, GA

Scripture quotations are from the following versions:

Dedication

This book is lovingly dedicated to my children, Heather,
James, Wendy and Jennifer, who sat around the kitchen table
as little children memorizing the Psalms.
And have shared these drawings in their teaching down
through the years. And to my dear husband, Ian,
who so lovingly proclaimed the Gospel, not only,
in the pulpit, but also, in our home.

Acknowledgments

With grateful appreciation to my dear friend and computer
whiz, Karen Hoerner, for her many hours of advising,
encouraging, changing, correcting and printing…
could not have done it without her.

Contents

Preface

The Psalms teach us that there is a way of blessedness in this world. For centuries they have comforted and encouraged us all the way from the battlefield to the hospital waiting room. They have ministered to those in the palace, the pew, the parlor and the prison. Because in them we find the full range of human experience and they become our own heart's cry.

God's Word tells us to keep our hearts with all diligence, "for out of it are the issues of life." (Proverbs 4:23) The Psalms help us to do that. In my "four score years" I have discovered some things for sure... when I grow spiritually dry and parched by the heat of this world, the psalms nourish and refresh my heart. When I lose my joy, they praise it back again. When I feel afraid and weak the psalms remind me that almighty God, Himself, is my refuge and strength. When I lose the wonder of it all they give me a fresh glimpse of His glory. Well...no wonder!... because we see Jesus in the psalms. Luke 24:44 says, "It is written in the Psalms concerning ME!" We feel his emotion in the Messianic Psalms, and the thrill of his soon return and millennial reign.

The psalms teach us to praise God, and since we are told that God inhabits the praise of his saints we are able to leave this dusty world and slip into His presence— moving from "howling to hallelujahs" as C. H. Spurgeon said.

I have had the great privilege of serving beside my husband in the ministry for sixty years. For forty of those years I have enjoyed teaching a bible study called Selah— an in depth study of the Psalms. These are some of the drawings from those years. They are my own special answer to a request I made to the Lord. As a busy wife and mother of four children it was difficult for me to find time to draw or paint just for my own enjoyment. So, I asked the Lord to help me organize my time and help me find a way to do that.

One day while studying my Psalm for that week a picture of a special truth formed in my mind, so I drew it and used it for my teaching. The same thing happened for the next study and for the next. One day I laughed as I realized that this was the sweet way God was answering my prayer. Each week I had the delightful assignment to combine my two special joys—the study of God's Word and the fun of illustrating a truth.

These illustrations would not mean much without the rich devotional thoughts from beloved writers of the past. So, I happily join with them in "rejoicing your heart".

—Esther Walker

Book One

Psalm 1-41

PSALM 1

OH THE JOYS OF THOSE WHO DO NOT FOLLOW EVIL-MENS ADVICE, WHO DO NOT HANG AROUND WITH SINNERS SCOFFING AT THE THINGS OF GOD! v.1

THE WAY OF HOLINESS — GOD'S WORD

THE WAY OF THE WORLD — MAN'S ADVICE

THE BROAD WAY

THE NARROW WAY

MAP
FOR THE LORD KNOWETH THE WAY OF THE RIGHTEOUS BUT THE WAY OF THE UNGODLY SHALL PERISH!

BUT THEY DELIGHT IN DOING EVERYTHING GOD WANTS THEM TO, AND DAY AND NIGHT ARE ALWAYS MEDITATING ON HIS LAWS AND THINKING OF WAYS TO FOLLOW HIM MORE CLOSELY. v.2

ENTER IN AT THE NARROW GATE; FOR WIDE IS THE GATE, AND BROAD IS THE WAY, THAT LEADETH TO DISTRUCTION, AND MANY THERE BE WHO GO IN THAT WAY; BECAUSE NARROW IS THE GATE, AND HARD IS THE WAY, WHICH LEADETH UNTO LIFE, AND FEW THERE BE THAT FIND IT.
MATT. 7:13,14

PSALM 2

You shall break them with a rod of iron; you shall dash them in pieces like potters' ware.

Now therefore, O you kings, act wisely; be instructed and warned, O you rulers of the earth!

Serve the Lord with reverent awe and worshipful fear; rejoice and be in high spirits with trembling lest you displease Him! v.v. 9-11

Yes! Jehovah has given to His anointed a rod of iron with which He shall break rebellious nations in pieces, and despite their imperial strength, they shall be as potters' vessels, easily dashed into shivers, when the rod of iron is in the hand of the Omnipotent Son of God...those who will not bend must break!

— C.H. Spurgeon

14

PSALM 3

MANY THERE BE WHICH SAY OF MY SOUL, THERE IS NO HELP FOR HIM IN GOD. ...SELAH...BUT THOU, O LORD, ART A SHIELD FOR ME; MY GLORY AND THE LIFTER OF MINE HEAD. I CRIED UNTO THE LORD WITH MY VOICE, AND HE HEARD ME OUT OF HIS HOLY HILL....SELAH.
I LAID ME DOWN AND SLEPT, I AWAKED; FOR THE LORD SUSTAINED ME! VV 2-5

O FOR GRACE TO SEE OUR FUTURE GLORY AMID PRESENT SHAME! INDEED THERE IS A PRESENT GLORY IN OUR AFFLICTIONS, IF WE COULD DISCERN IT; FOR IT IS NO SMALL THING TO HAVE FELLOWSHIP WITH CHRIST IN HIS SUFFERINGS.
THOUGH I HANG MY HEAD IN SORROW, I SHALL VERY SOON LIFT IT UP IN JOY AND THANKSGIVING. WHAT A DIVINE TRIO OF MERCIES IS CONTAINED IN THIS VERSE! DEFENSE FOR THE DEFENSELESS, GLORY FOR THE DESPISED, AND JOY FOR THE COMFORTLESS! — C.H. SPURGEON

15

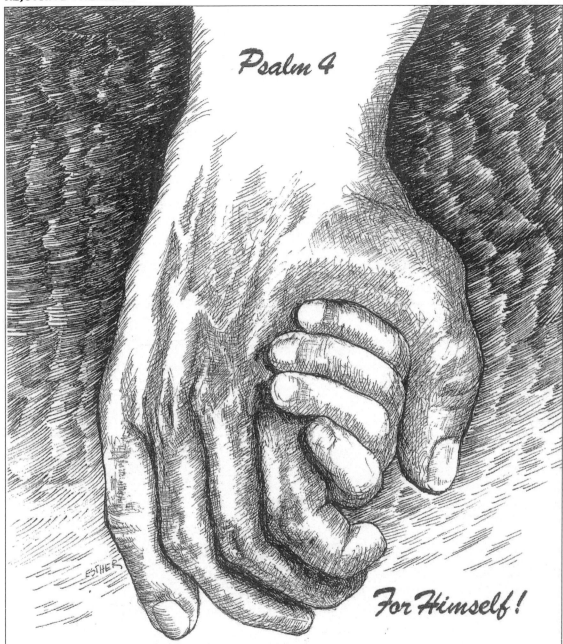

Psalm 4

For Himself!

BUT KNOW THAT THE LORD HATH SET APART HIM THAT IS GODLY FOR HIMSELF: THE LORD WILL HEAR WHEN I CRY UNTO HIM. STAND IN AWE, AND SIN NOT: COMMUNE WITH YOUR OWN HEART UPON YOUR BED... AND BE STILL. SELAH   vv.3,4

MY VOICE SHALT THOU HEAR IN THE MORNING, O LORD; IN THE MORNING
WILL I DIRECT MY PRAYER UNTO THEE, AND WILL LOOK UP. V. 3. KJV

STILL, STILL WITH THEE, WHEN PURPLE MORNING BREAKETH, WHEN THE BIRD
WAKETH, AND THE SHADOWS FLEE; FAIRER THAN MORNING, LOVELIER THAN DAYLIGHT,
DAWNS THE SWEET CONSCIOUSNESS... I AM WITH THEE!

ALONE WITH THEE,
AMID THE MYSTIC SHADOWS,
THE SOLEMN HUSH OF
NATURE NEWLY BORN;
ALONE WITH THEE
IN BREATHLESS ADORATION,
IN THE CALM DEW AND
FRESHNESS OF THE MORN.
    — HARRIET B. STOWE

PSALM 5

PSALM 6

DEPART FROM ME, ALL YE WORKERS OF INIQUITY; FOR THE LORD HATH HEARD THE VOICE OF MY WEEPING. THE LORD HATH HEARD MY SUPPLICATION; THE LORD WILL RECEIVE MY PRAYER.

V.V. 8,9

WHAT A FRIEND WE HAVE IN JESUS, ALL OUR SINS AND GRIEFS TO BEAR! WHAT A PRIVILEGE TO CARRY EVERYTHING TO GOD IN PRAYER! OH, WHAT PEACE WE OFTEN FORFEIT, OH, WHAT NEEDLESS PAIN WE BEAR, ALL BECAUSE WE DO NOT CARRY EVERYTHING TO GOD IN PRAYER!

HAVE WE TRIALS AND TEMPTATIONS? IS THERE TROUBLE ANYWHERE? WE SHOULD NEVER BE DISCOURAGED; TAKE IT TO THE LORD IN PRAYER. CAN WE FIND A FRIEND SO FAITHFUL WHO WILL ALL OUR SORROWS SHARE? JESUS KNOWS OUR EVERY WEAKNESS, TAKE IT TO THE LORD IN PRAYER!

—JOSEPH SCRIVEN · 1819-1866

18

O Lord my God, in thee do I put my trust: save me
from all them that persecute me, and deliver me:
lest he tear my soul like a lion, rending it in pieces,
while there is none to deliver. Vv.1,2
My defence is of God, which saveth the upright in heart.
V.10

Be sober, be vigilant; because your adversary
the devil, as a roaring lion, walketh about,
seeking whom he may devour.
Whom resist stedfast in the faith,
knowing that the same afflictions
are accomplished
in your brethren
that are in the world.
1 Peter 5:8,9

PSALM 7

19

PSALM 8

O Lord our Lord, how excellent is thy name in all the earth!
who hast set thy glory above the heavens. When I consider
thy heavens, the work of thy fingers, the moon and the stars,
which thou hast ordained; what is man, that thou art
mindful of him? And the son of man, that thou visitest him?
For thou hast made him a little lower than the angels,
and hast crowned him with glory and honour.
O Lord our Lord, how excellent is thy name in all the earth!
vv. 1, 3–5, 9

PSALM 9

I WILL PRAISE THEE, O LORD,
WITH MY WHOLE HEART; I WILL SHOW FORTH
ALL THY MARVELOUS WORKS. I WILL BE GLAD AND REJOICE IN THEE;
I WILL SING PRAISE TO THY NAME, O THOU MOST HIGH.   V.V. 1, 2
                                                            KJV

QUIET TENSION IS NOT TRUST, IT IS SIMPLY COMPRESSED ANXIETY! TOO OFTEN WE THINK WE ARE TRUSTING WHEN WE ARE MERELY CONTROLLING OUR PANIC. TRUE FAITH GIVES NOT ONLY A CALM EXTERIOR BUT A QUIET HEART.

MISS. AMY CARMICHAEL GIVES A BEAUTIFUL ILLUSTRATION FROM NATURE OF THIS KIND OF TRUST. THE SUN BIRD, ONE OF THE TINIEST BIRDS, A NATIVE OF INDIA, BUILDS A PENDANT NEST, HANGING IT BY FOUR FRAIL THREADS, GENERALLY FROM A SPRAY OF VALARIS. IT IS A DELICATE WORK OF ART, WITH ITS ROOF AND TINY PORCH, WHICH A SPLASH OF WATER OR A CHILD'S TOUCH MIGHT DESTROY. MISS. CARMICHAEL TELLS HOW SHE SAW A LITTLE SUN BIRD BUILDING SUCH A NEST JUST BEFORE THE MONSOON SEASON, AND FELT THAT FOR ONCE BIRD WISDOM HAD FAILED; FOR HOW COULD SUCH A DELICATE STRUCTURE, IN SUCH AN EXPOSED SITUATION, WEATHER THE WINDS AND THE TORRENTIAL RAINS? THE MONSOON BROKE, AND FROM HER WINDOW SHE WATCHED THE NEST SWAYING WITH THE BRANCHES IN THE WIND. THEN SHE PERCEIVED THAT THE NEST HAD BEEN PLACED THAT THE LEAVES IMMEDIATLY ABOVE IT FORMED LITTLE GUTTERS WHICH CARRIED THE WATER AWAY FROM THE NEST.

THERE SAT THE SUN BIRD, WITH ITS TINY HEAD RESTING ON HER PORCH, AND WHENEVER A DROP OF WATER FELL ON HER LONG, CURVED BEAK, SHE SUCKED IT IN AS IF IT WERE NECTAR... THE STORM RAGED FURIOUSLY, BUT THE SUN BIRD SAT QUIET AND UNAFRAID HATCHING HER TINY EGGS... WE HAVE A MORE SUBSTANTIAL REST FOR HEAD AND HEART THAN THE SUN BIRD'S PORCH! WE HAVE THE PROMISES OF GOD!   J.C. MACAULAY

PSALM 10

The wicked in his pride doth persecute the poor;
Let them be taken in the devices that they have
    imagined. v2
  He lieth in wait secretly as a lion in his den;
He lieth in wait to catch the poor; he doth catch
the poor, when he draweth him into his net. v9
    Arise O Lord, O God lift up thine hand
Forget not the humble! v12

BE SOBER, BE VIGILENT BECAUSE YOUR
ADVERSARY, THE DEVIL, AS A ROARING LION,
WALKETH ABOUT — SEEKING WHOM HE MAY
DEVOUR! 1PETER 5:8

NEVER NEGLECT TO ABIDE IN YOUR STRONG
FORTRESS — CHRIST.
  KEEP WITH THE FLOCK OF GOD. NOURISH
YOUR SOUL WITH THE WORD OF GOD. THAT
YOU MAY BE HEALTHY AND STRONG.
GIRD ON THE WHOLE ARMOUR OF GOD.
RESIST THE FIRST INSIGNIFICANT
ADVANCES OF THE FOE.
  BE STEADFAST IN THE FAITH,
  RESIST THE DEVIL AND HE
    WILL FLEE FROM YOU!
      GO INTO BATTLE ASSURED
OF SUCCESS.

"THEY OVER CAME HIM
  BY THE BLOOD
  OF THE LAMB"
THIS IS YOUR
BATTLE CRY...
JESUS SAVES,
JESUS SAVES,
JESUS
SAVES!

F. B MEYER

PSALM 11

THE LORD IS IN HIS HOLY TEMPLE,
THE LORD'S THRONE IS IN HEAVEN;
HIS EYES BEHOLD, HIS EYELIDS TRY
THE CHILDREN OF MEN.   V 4.

THE GOD OF THE BELIEVER IS NEVER FAR
FROM HIM; HE IS NOT MERELY THE GOD OF THE
MOUNTAIN FASTNESSES, BUT OF THE DANGEROUS
VALLEYS AND BATTLE PLAINS. THE HEAVENS ARE
ABOVE OUR HEADS IN ALL REGIONS OF THE EARTH,
AND SO IS THE LORD EVER NEAR TO US IN EVERY
STATE AND CONDITION. THIS IS WHY WE SHOULD NOT
ADOPT THE VILE SUGGESTIONS OF DISTRUST. THERE
IS ONE WHO PLEADS HIS PRECIOUS BLOOD IN OUR
BEHALF IN THE TEMPLE ABOVE, AND THERE IS ONE
UPON THE THRONE WHO IS NEVER DEAF TO THE
INTERCESSION OF HIS SON. WHY THEN SHOULD WE
FEAR? WHAT PLOTS CAN MEN DEVISE WHICH JESUS
WILL NOT DISCOVER? SATAN HAS DOUBTLESS DESIRED
TO HAVE US, THAT HE MAY SIFT US AS WHEAT, BUT
JESUS IS IN THE TEMPLE PRAYING FOR US, AND
HOW CAN OUR FAITH FAIL?
          — C.H. SPURGEON

ESTHER

PSALM 12

HELP, LORD;

FOR THE GODLY MAN CEASETH,
FOR THE FAITHFUL FAILS FROM AMONG
THE CHILDREN OF MEN. THEY SPEAK VANITY
EVERYONE WITH HIS NEIGHBOR;
WITH FLATTERING LIPS AND WITH A
DOUBLE HEART DO THEY SPEAK. Vv 1-2

THE PRESENT TIMES ALWAYS APPEAR
TO BE PECULIARLY DANGEROUS,
BECAUSE THEY ARE NEAREST TO OUR
ANXIOUS GAZE, AND WHATEVER EVILS
ARE RIFE ARE SURE TO BE OBSERVED,
WHILE THE FAULTS OF THE PAST AGES
ARE FURTHER OFF AND ARE MORE
EASILY OVERLOOKED....
TOTAL DESTRUCTION SHALL OVERWHELM
THE LOVERS OF FLATTERY AND PRIDE,
BUT MEANWHILE HOW THEY
HECTOR AND FUME! WELL DID THE APOSTLE
CALL THEM' RAGING WAVES OF THE SEA,
FOAMING OUT THEIR OWN SHAME
THE DARKEST HOURS OF THE CHURCH'S NIGHT
ARE THOSE WHICH PRECEDE THE BREAK OF DAY.
MAN'S EXTREMITY IS GOD'S OPPORTUNITY!
JESUS WILL COME TO DELIVER
JUST WHEN HIS NEEDY ONES SHALL SIGH,
AS IF ALL HOPE HAD GONE FOREVER.
C. H. SPURGEON

PSALM 13

BUT I HAVE TRUSTED IN THY MERCY; MY HEART SHALL REJOICE IN THY SALVATION... ... I WILL SING UNTO THE LORD, BECAUSE HE HATH DEALT BOUNTIFULLY WITH ME!

v.v. 5,6

LO, THE RAIN IS OVER AND GONE, AND THE TIME OF THE SINGING OF BIRDS IS COME. THE MERCY-SEAT HAS SO REFRESHED THE POOR WEEPER, THAT HE CLEARS HIS THROAT FOR A SONG... IT IS WORTHY TO BE OBSERVED THAT THE JOY IS ALL THE GREATER BECAUSE OF THE PREVIOUS SORROW, ALL THE MORE DELIGHTFUL REMEMBERING THE PRECEDING TEMPEST. C.H. SPURGEON

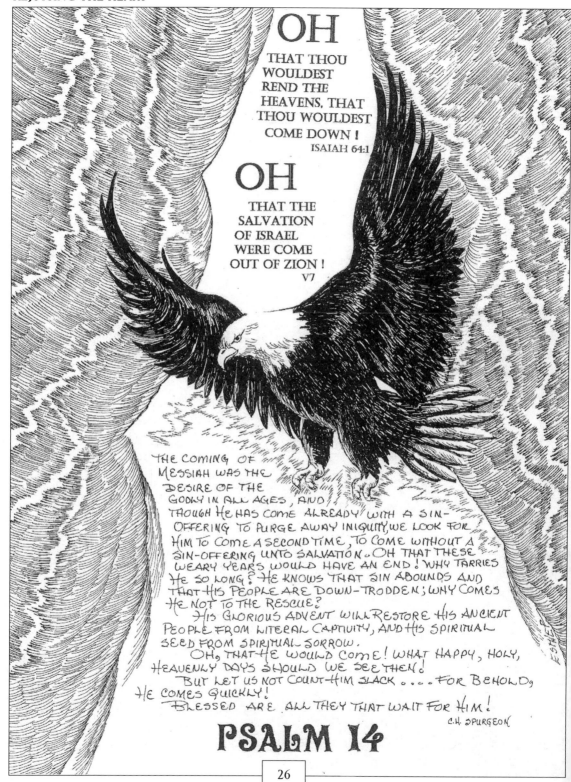

OH

THAT THOU WOULDEST REND THE HEAVENS, THAT THOU WOULDEST COME DOWN !

ISAIAH 64:1

OH

THAT THE SALVATION OF ISRAEL WERE COME OUT OF ZION !

V7

THE COMING OF MESSIAH WAS THE DESIRE OF THE GODLY IN ALL AGES, AND THOUGH HE HAS COME ALREADY WITH A SIN-OFFERING TO PURGE AWAY INIQUITY, WE LOOK FOR HIM TO COME A SECOND TIME, TO COME WITHOUT A SIN-OFFERING UNTO SALVATION. OH THAT THESE WEARY YEARS WOULD HAVE AN END! WHY TARRIES HE SO LONG? HE KNOWS THAT SIN ABOUNDS AND THAT HIS PEOPLE ARE DOWN-TRODDEN; WHY COMES HE NOT TO THE RESCUE?

HIS GLORIOUS ADVENT WILL RESTORE HIS ANCIENT PEOPLE FROM LITERAL CAPTIVITY, AND HIS SPIRITUAL SEED FROM SPIRITUAL SORROW.

OH, THAT HE WOULD COME! WHAT HAPPY, HOLY, HEAVENLY DAYS SHOULD WE SEE THEN!

BUT LET US NOT COUNT HIM SLACK .... FOR BEHOLD, HE COMES QUICKLY!

BLESSED ARE ALL THEY THAT WAIT FOR HIM!

C.H. SPURGEON

PSALM 14

PSALM 15

LORD, WHO SHALL ABIDE IN THY TABERNACLE? WHO SHALL DWELL IN THY HOLY HILL? V. 1

THIS HOLY SOUL WAS NOT CONTENT TO STAND IN THE OUTER COURT WITHOUT THE SACRED TENT AND HE COVETED TO ENTER WHERE THE HIGH PRIEST ENTERED, AND TO LIVE THERE. IT WAS IMPOSSIBLE THEN, THE WAY INTO THE HOLIEST WAS NOT MADE MANIFEST. HOW MARVELOUSLY DIFFERENT OUR EXPERIENCE MAY BE! WE HAVE BOLDNESS TO ENTER INTO THE HOLY PLACE, AND REMAIN THERE, BY THE BLOOD OF JESUS, AND BY THE ENABLINGS OF HIS PRIESTHOOD, WE MAY SPEND OUR ENTIRE LIVES UNDER THE CONSCIENCE OF THE PRESENCE AND FAVOR OF GOD!

IT IS WORTH ANY SACRIFICE TO MAINTAIN THIS HABIT OF IN-DWELLING THE MOST HOLY PLACE ASK THAT IT MAY BECOME YOUR SECOND NATURE. THE LORD JESUS WILL SECURE THIS, SINCE HE WAS APPOINTED FOR US IN THINGS THAT PERTAIN TO GOD!
—F.B MEYER

PSALM 16

Therefore my heart is glad , and my glory rejoiceth:
my flesh also shall rest in hope. For thou wilt not leave
my soul in hell; neither wilt thou suffer thine Holy One
to see corruption. Thou wilt shew me the path of life: in thy
presence is fullness of joy; at thy right hand there are pleasures
for evermore. Vv. 9-11

Whenever you are stepping down into the dark, unable to see a
hand's-breath before you, and just letting the foot fall from step to
step-It may be because of some act of obedience to conscience or because
you are called to enter the unknown and untried, or even death itself—
Cheer your heart with this holy psalm. God will never desert the soul
that absolutely honours and obeys Him. His way leads to the light through
the dark, to the deathless through death, to the abounding fruit—bearing,
through desertion and loneliness. How lonely the vine-stock is through the
winter! Follow Him, He will show you.

""She is sinking very fast," whispered an attendant in the dying
chamber of a godly woman. "No, No," was the quick response of
the departing saint, who had overheard the words. "No; I am not
sinking; I am in the arms of my saviour." --F.B. myer

PSALM 17

Hear the right, O Lord, attend unto my cry, Give ear unto my prayer, that goeth not out of feigned lips. V.1.

Hold up my goings in thy paths, that my footsteps slip not. V.5

Precious Lord, take my hand,
    Lead me on, help me stand —
I am tired, I am weak, I am worn,
    Thro' the storm, thro' the night,
Lead me on to the light —
    Take my hand, precious Lord,
Lead me home.

When my way grows drear,
    Precious Lord, linger near —
When my life is almost gone,
    Hear my cry, hear my call,
Hold my hand lest I fall —
    Take my hand, precious Lord,
Lead me home!

— Thomas Dorsey

For I, the Lord thy God, will hold thy right hand, saying unto thee, Fear not.... I will help thee! Isaiah 41:13

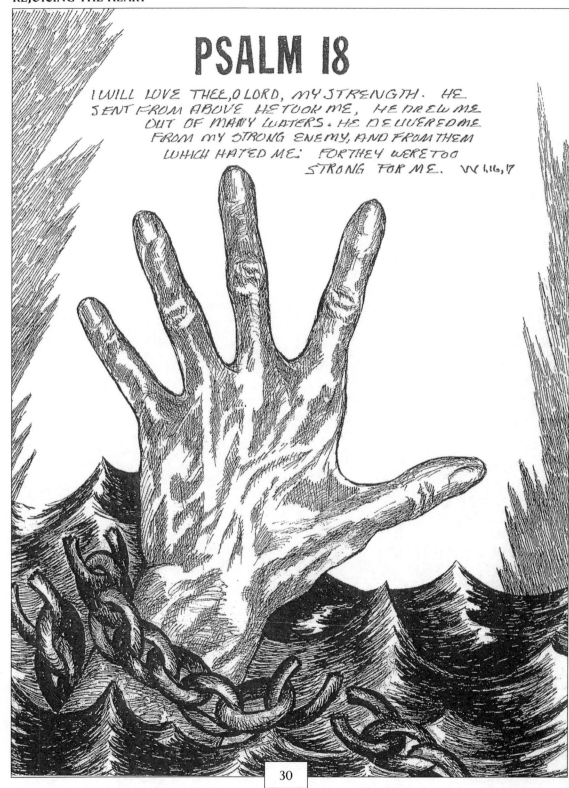

PSALM 18

I WILL LOVE THEE, O LORD, MY STRENGTH. HE
SENT FROM ABOVE HE TOOK ME, HE DREW ME
OUT OF MANY WATERS. HE DELIVERED ME
FROM MY STRONG ENEMY, AND FROM THEM
WHICH HATED ME: FORTHEY WERE TOO
STRONG FOR ME. VV 1,16,17

PSALM 19

THE HEAVENS DECLARE THE GLORY OF GOD, AND THE FIRMAMENT SHOWETH HIS HANDIWORK. v.1
THE LAW OF THE LORD IS PERFECT, CONVERTING THE SOUL; THE TESTIMONY OF THE LORD IS SURE, MAKING WISE THE SIMPLE. v.7

EVERY MOMENT GOD'S EXISTENCE, POWER, WISDOM, AND GOODNESS ARE BEING SOUNDED ABROAD BY THE HEAVENLY HERALDS WHICH SHINE UPON US FROM ABOVE... HE WHO WOULD IMAGINE INFINITY MUST PEER INTO THE BOUNDLESS EXPANSE; HE WHO DESIRES TO SEE DIVINE WISDOM SHOULD CONSIDER THE BALANCING OF THE ORBS... AND HE WHO WOULD ATTAIN SOME CONCEPTION OF DIVINE POWER, GREATNESS, AND MAJESTY MUST ESTIMATE THE FORCES OF ATTRACTION, THE MAGNITUDE OF THE FIXED STARS AND THE BRIGHTNESS OF THE WHOLE CELESTIAL TRAIN. IT IS NOT MERELY GLORY THAT THE HEAVENS DECLARE... BUT THE GLORY OF GOD! FOR THEY DELIVER TO US UNANSWERABLE ARGUMENTS FOR A CONSCIOUS, INTELLIGENT, PLANNING, CONTROLLING, AND PRESIDING CREATOR!
        YET FOR ALL THIS, TO WHAT AVAIL IS THE LOUDEST DECLARATION TO A DEAF MAN? GOD THE HOLY GHOST MUST ILLUMINATE US OR ALL THE SUNS IN THE MILKY WAY NEVER WILL!
        -C.H. SPURGEON

31

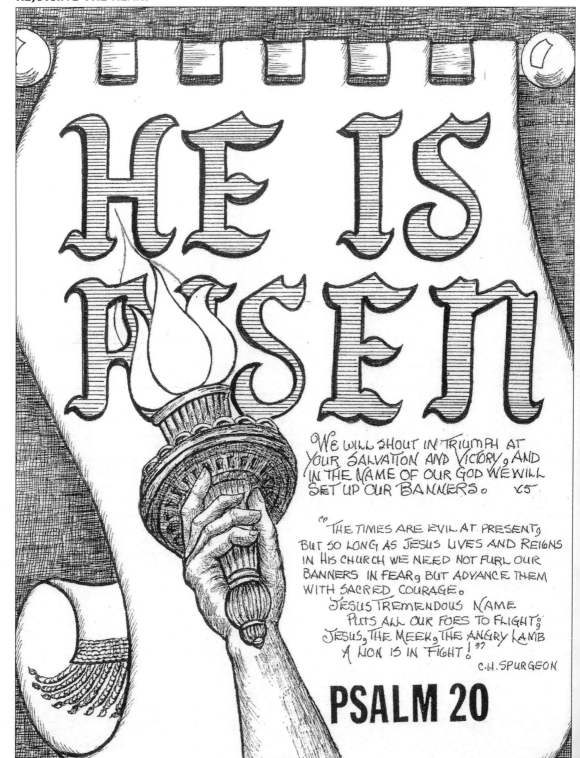

HE IS RISEN

WE WILL SHOUT IN TRIUMPH AT YOUR SALVATION AND VICTORY, AND IN THE NAME OF OUR GOD WE WILL SET UP OUR BANNERS. v5

"THE TIMES ARE EVIL AT PRESENT, BUT SO LONG AS JESUS LIVES AND REIGNS IN HIS CHURCH WE NEED NOT FURL OUR BANNERS IN FEAR, BUT ADVANCE THEM WITH SACRED COURAGE.

JESUS TREMENDOUS NAME
PUTS ALL OUR FOES TO FLIGHT,
JESUS, THE MEEK, THE ANGRY LAMB
A LION IS IN FIGHT!"

C.H. SPURGEON

PSALM 20

PSALM 21

THE KING SHALL JOY IN THY STRENGTH, O LORD; AND IN THY
SALVATION HOW GREATLY SHALL HE REJOICE! THOU HAST GIVEN HIM
HIS HEART'S DESIRE, AND HAST NOT WITHHELD THE REQUEST OF HIS
LIPS. SELAH . FOR THOU DOST MEET HIM WITH THE BLESSINGS OF GOODNESS
THOU HAST SET A CROWN OF PURE GOLD ON HIS HEAD.
VV. 1-3

ESTHER

BUT UNTO THE SON HE SAITH, THY THRONE OH GOD, IS FOREVER AND EVER;
A SEPTRE OF RIGHTEOUSNESS IS THE SEPTRE OF THY KINGDOM . . . .
AND THOU, O LORD, IN THE BEGINNING, HAST LAID THE FOUNDATION OF
THE EARTH; AND THE HEAVENS ARE THE WORK OF THY HANDS!
HEBREWS 1:8,10

PSALM 22

MY GOD, MY GOD, WHY HAST THOU FORSAKEN ME?
WHY ART THOU SO FAR FROM HELPING ME, AND FROM THE
WORDS OF MY ROARING? V1

AND AT THE NINTH HOUR JESUS CRIED WITH A
LOUD VOICE, SAYING, ELOI, ELOI, LAMA SABACHTHAN?
WHICH IS, BEING INTERPRETED, MY GOD, MY GOD,
WHY HAST THOU FORSAKEN ME?

MARK 15:34

"HE COULD HAVE CALLED TEN THOUSAND ANGELS
TO DESTROY THE WORLD, AND SET HIM FREE
HE COULD HAVE CALLED TEN THOUSAND ANGELS,
BUT HE DIED ALONE ..... FOR YOU AND ME!"

34

PSALM 23

The Lord is my Shepherd, I shall not want. v1.

UP FROM THE MOUNTAINS THUNDER RIV'N,
   AND UP FROM THE ROCKY STEEP;
THERE CAME A GLAD CRY TO THE GATES OF HEAVEN
   "REJOICE! I HAVE FOUND MY SHEEP."
AND THE ANGELS ECHO AROUND THE THRONE
   "REJOICE! FOR THE LORD BRINGS BACK HIS OWN!"

PSALM 24

LIFT UP YOUR HEADS, O YE GATES; EVEN LIFT THEM UP, YE EVERLASTING DOORS, AND THE KING OF GLORY SHALL COME IN... WHO IS THIS KING OF GLORY? THE LORD OF HOSTS — HE IS THE KING OF GLORY. SELAH VS. 9, 10

REV. 5:6,7 12,13

But the most vital fulfillment is when the heart opens to receive Him, and He enters, to go out no more, and to hold it against all comers. Oh, beaten and baffled saint, it is impossible for thee to fail when Jesus, all-victorious, garrisons thy heart! He is strong and mighty. Dost thou want strength? It is in the strong Son of God. Dost thou want might? He is all-mighty. Dost thou want deliverance from thy foes? He is mighty in battle. F.B. Meyers

PSALM 25

Shew me thy ways, O Lord; teach me
thy paths.Lead me in thy truth,
and teach me: for thou art the
God of my salvation; on thee do I
wait all the day. Remember not
the sins of my youth, nor
my transgressions: according
to thy mercy remember
thou me for thy
goodness' sake, O Lord.
Vv 4,5,7

HE LEADETH ME! O BLESSED THOUGHT!
O WORDS WITH HEAVENLY COMFORT FRAUGHT!
WHATEVER I DO, WHEREVER I BE, STILL 'TIS GOD'S
HAND THAT LEADETH ME!
SOMETIMES 'MID SCENES OF DEEPEST GLOOM,
SOMETIMES WHERE EDEN'S BOWERS BLOOM, BY WATERS STILL, O'ER
TROUBLED SEA, STILL 'TIS HIS HAND THAT LEADETH ME!
LORD, I WOULD CLASP THY HAND IN MINE, NOR EVER
MURMUR NOR REPINE, CONTENT WHATEVER LOT I SEE, SINCE 'TIS THY HAND
THAT LEADETH ME!
HE LEADETH ME, HE LEADETH ME, BY HIS OWN HAND
HE LEADETH ME; HIS FAITHFUL FOLLOWER I WOULD BE....FOR BY HIS
HAND HE LEADETH ME!

—— JOSEPH H. GILMORE
1834-1918

37

PSALM 26

But as for me, I will walk in mine integrity: redeem me, and be merciful unto me.
My foot standeth in an even place: in the congregations will I bless the Lord.
vv. 11,12

SAINTS OFTEN SING THEMSELVES INTO HAPPINESS. THE EVEN PLACE UPON WHICH OUR FOOT STANDS IS THE SURE, COVENANT FAITHFULNESS, ETERNAL PROMISE AND IMMUTABLE OATH OF THE LORD OF HOSTS; THERE IS NO FEAR OF FALLING FROM THIS SOLID BASIS, OR OF ITS BEING REMOVED FROM UNDER US. ESTABLISHED IN CHRIST JESUS, BY BEING VITALLY UNITED TO HIM, WE HAVE NOTHING LEFT TO OCCUPY OUR THOUGHTS BUT THE PRAISES OF GOD. AS FOR SLANDERERS, LET THEM HOWL!
— C.H. SPURGEON

FOR THE SPIRIT WHICH YOU HAVE RECEIVED IS NOT A SPIRIT OF SLAVERY TO PUT YOU ONCE MORE IN BONDAGE TO FEAR, BUT YOU HAVE RECEIVED THE SPIRIT OF ADOPTION – THE SPIRIT PRODUCING SONSHIP – IN THE BLISS OF WHICH WE CRY, ABBA! THAT IS ... FATHER! DADDY!
ROMANS 8:15 AMP

THE LORD IS MY LIGHT AND MY SALVATION; WHOM SHALL I FEAR? THE LORD IS THE STRENGTH OF MY LIFE; OF WHOM SHALL I BE AFRAID?
ONE THING HAVE I DESIRED OF THE LORD, AND THAT WILL I SEEK AFTER; THAT I MAY DWELL IN THE HOUSE OF THE LORD ALL THE DAYS OF MY LIFE, TO BEHOLD THE BEAUTY OF THE LORD, AND TO INQUIRE IN HIS TEMPLE.
FOR IN THE TIME OF TROUBLE HE SHALL HIDE ME IN HIS PAVILION; IN THE SECRET OF HIS TABERNACLE SHALL HE HIDE ME!
V.V. 1, 4, 5

PSALM 27

PSALM 28

Blessed be the Lord, because he hath heard the voice of my supplications. The Lord is my strength and my shield; my heart trusteth in him, and I am helped: therefore my heart greatly rejoiceth: and with my song will I praise him. The Lord is their strength, and he is the saving strength of his anointed.

Save thy people, and bless thine inheritance: feed them also, and lift them up for ever.   vv. 6-9

"BEAR THEM UP FOREVER." THE GOOD SHEPHERD BORE HIS FLOCK THROUGH THE DESERT, AND CARRIED THEM ALL THE DAYS OF OLD, IT IS AS EASY FOR HIM TO BEAR A FLOCK, AS A SINGLE LAMB. JESUS DOES NOT SIMPLY LEAD US TO GREEN PASTURES AND STILL WATERS, HE BEARS US, AND BEARS US UP . . . . NEVER TIRING, NEVER CEASING FOR A MOMMENT HIS SHEPHERD-CARE. ARE YOU DEPRESSED TODAY? ARE THERE STRONG INFLUENCES DRAGGING YOU DOWN? DOES YOUR SOUL CLEAVE TO THE DUST? LET THOSE STRONG ARMS AND THAT TENDER BREAST LIFT YOU UP FOREVER."   — F.B. MEYER

"CARRY THEM IN THINE ARMS ON EARTH, AND THEN LIFT THEM INTO THY BOSOM IN HEAVEN!"
                                                    — C.H. SPURGEON

PSALM 29

Give unto the Lord, O ye mighty, give unto the Lord glory and strength. The voice of the Lord is upon the waters: the God of glory thundereth: the Lord is upon many waters. The voice of the Lord is powerful: the voice of the Lord is full of majesty. The voice of the Lord divideth the flames of fire. vv. 1, 3, 4, 7

...and in his temple doth every one speak of his GLORY. v.9

GLORY ... GLORY ... GLORY!

MANY STORMS ARE SWEEPING THROUGH THE WORLD JUST NOW. OUR STANDPOINT FOR WATCHING THEM MUST BE GOD'S PRESENCE-CHAMBER. SOMEHOW, EVERYTHING THAT HAS BEEN, IS, AND SHALL BE; ALL THAT SEEMS STARTLING AND DREADFUL; ALL THAT EXCITES FEAR AND FOREBODING — SHALL CONDUCE TO THE GLORY OF GOD. WAIT, O CHILD OF GOD, IN PATIENT TRUST; JEHOVAH IS KING, AND HE SHALL SIT AS KING FOREVER!

— F.B. MEYER

PSALM 30

WEEPING MAY ENDURE FOR A NIGHT...BUT JOY COMETH IN THE MORNING.
v5

Now see, the morning breaks! Who is this hurrying up the hill, and knocking at the door? Hark to his joyous shout! Who is this? Ah! It is Joy, the child of the morning light! The first born of resurrection! And he comes not as a lodger, but as the Lord and Master of life, to abide forever. Oh, welcome him in the name of the Lord, and throw open each chamber and each closet in your heart, that all may be filled with Joy unspeakable and full of glory. And as he enters, sorrow and sighing flee away. They have passed out at the back as he came in at the front.

Joy in the morning at the resurrection of Jesus; Joy in the coming of the Saviour for His bride; Joy as the Millennium breaks on the world; Joy when the eternal day comes to gladden those who have drunk of Christ's sorrow, and shall share His bliss!

— F.B. MEYER

PSALM 31

OH LORD... HELP ME!

... BE FOR ME A GREAT ROCK OF SAFETY FROM MY FOES. YES! YOU ARE MY ROCK AND MY FORTRESS; HONOR YOUR NAME BY LEADING ME OUT OF THIS PERIL. PULL ME FROM THE TRAP MY ENEMIES HAVE SET FOR ME. FOR YOU ALONE ARE STRONG ENOUGH. INTO YOUR HAND I COMMIT MY SPIRIT... YOU HAVE RESCUED ME, O GOD WHO KEEPS HIS PROMISES.   V.V. 2-6

WELL MAY THE ENLIGHTENED SOUL ADORE SUCH A GOD! THE WONDROUS AND INFINITE PERFECTIONS OF SUCH A BEING CALL FOR FERVENT WORSHIP......... WELL MAY THE SAINT TRUST SUCH A GOD! HE IS WORTHY OF IMPLICIT CONFIDENCE. NOTHING IS TOO HARD FOR HIM. IF GOD WERE STINTED IN MIGHT AND HAD A LIMIT TO HIS STRENGTH WE MIGHT WELL DESPAIR. BUT SEEING THAT HE IS CLOTHED WITH OMNIPOTENCE, NO PRAYER IS TOO HARD FOR HIM TO ANSWER, NO NEED TOO GREAT FOR HIM TO SUPPLY, NO PASSION TOO STRONG FOR HIM TO SUBDUE; NO TEMPTATION TOO POWERFUL FOR HIM TO DELIVER FROM, NO MISERY TOO DEEP FOR HIM TO RELIEVE. "THE LORD IS THE STRENGTH OF MY LIFE; OF WHOM SHALL I BE AFRAID? (PS.27:1)" NOW UNTO HIM WHO IS ABLE TO DO EXCEEDING ABUNDANTLY ABOVE ALL THAT WE ASK OR THINK, ACCORDING TO THE POWER THAT WORKETH IN US, UNTO HIM BE GLORY! EPH 3:20,21
— ARTHUR PINK

PSALM 32

Be ye not as the horse, or as the mule, which have no understanding; whose mouth must be held in with bit and bridle, lest they come near unto thee. v 9

"THE HORSE HAS A NATURE WHICH MAKES IT WANT TO RUN AWAY; THE MULE HAS A NATURE WHICH MAKES IT REFUSE TO MOVE. THE LORD DOES NOT WISH TO HANDLE US LIKE A DUMB BEAST WITH A WILD AND WILLFUL NATURE. HE DOES NOT WANT TO HAVE TO BRIDLE US. THE ONLY WAY TO GOVERN A BEAST OF BURDEN IS TO PUT A BIT IN ITS MOUTH AND A BRIDLE ON ITS HEAD; THEN IT HAS TO DO WHAT ITS MASTER WANTS. GOD WOULD HAVE US SHOW MORE SENSE THAN THAT!"
—JOHN PHILLIPS

I will instruct thee and teach thee in the way which thou shalt go: I will guide thee with mine eye. Be glad in the Lord, and rejoice, ye righteous: and shout for joy, all ye that are upright in heart. vv 8, 11

"IF THE LORD IS TO GUIDE US WITH HIS EYE, IT MEANS THAT WE MUST STAY CLOSE TO HIM. A PERSON CANNOT GIVE ANOTHER PERSON A WARNING LOOK, OR A WARM LOOK, OR A WELCOMING LOOK IF HE IS IN CHICAGO AND THE FRIEND IN ATLANTA. THEY MUST BE WITHIN SIGHT OF EACH OTHER. NOR CAN HE GUIDE WITH HIS EYE IF HIS FRIEND IS NOT LOOKING AT HIM. HOW DESPERATELY WE NEED GUIDANCE IN OUR JOURNEY THROUGH THIS WORLD!

LET US SEE TO IT THAT WE ALLOW OUR LORD TO GUIDE US BY KEEPING OUR BIBLES OPEN AND OUR EYES EVER LOOKING TO HIM..... HE WILL MAKE IT PLAIN WHAT WE OUGHT TO DO!"
—JOHN PHILLIPS

PSALM 33

Rejoice

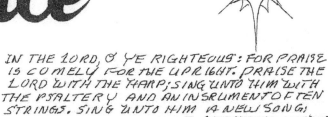

IN THE LORD, O YE RIGHTEOUS: FOR PRAISE IS COMELY FOR THE UPRIGHT. PRAISE THE LORD WITH THE HARP; SING UNTO HIM WITH THE PSALTERY AND AN INSTRUMENT OF TEN STRINGS. SING UNTO HIM A NEW SONG;

"WAIT FOR THE LORD!"

OUR SOUL WAITETH FOR THE LORD FOR HE IS OUR HELP AND OUR SHIELD. V. 20 —— WAITING SEEMS TO BE THE AGELONG LOT OF GOD'S PEOPLE. IT OFTEN SEEMS AS THOUGH OUR PRAYERS GO UNANSWERED, THAT GOD TAKES A LONG TIME TO ACT... BUT HELP IS ON THE WAY. GOD WORKS HIS OWN MYSTERIOUS TIMETABLE. HE HAS NOT FORGOTTEN US. WE CAN BE SURE OF THAT. HIS INTERFERENCE IN HISTORY WHEN HE SENT HIS SON TO REDEEM WAS RIGHT ON TIME. HELP IS ON THE WAY.
—JOHN PHILLIPS

PLAY SKILLFULLY WITH A LOUD NOISE. FOR THE WORD OF THE LORD IS RIGHT; AND ALL HIS WORKS ARE DONE IN TRUTH. HE LOVETH RIGHTEOUSNESS AND JUDGEMENT; THE EARTH IS FULL OF THE GOODNESS OF THE LORD! VV 1-5

45

PSALM 34

THE ANGEL OF THE LORD ENCAMPETH ROUND ABOUT
THEM THAT FEAR HIM AND DELIVERETH THEM.
V. 7

IF WE HAD OTHER, LARGER EYES THAN OURS WE WOULD SEE ALL ABOUT THE AIR, THE MIGHTY COUNTLESS HOSTS OF HELL — THOSE FEARFUL PRINCIPAL-ITIES AND POWERS ... BUT WE WOULD SEE TOO, THE RESPLENDENT RANKS OF THE SHINING ONES, THE MIGHTY ANGELS OF GOD DRAWN UP IN BATTLE ARRAY TO PRESERVE AND PROTECT THE SAINTS OF GOD. ABOVE AND BEYOND THEM ALL IS THE GLORIOUS ANGEL OF THE LORD HIMSELF!
— JOHN PHILLIPS

PSALM 35

Plead my cause, O Lord, with them
that strive with me: fight against
them that fight against me.
Take hold of shield and buckler,
and stand up for mine help. Draw
out also the spear, and stop the way
against them that persecute me: ......
And my soul shall be joyful in
the Lord: it shall rejoice in his salvation.
VV 1-3,9

SAINTS ARE TOO DEAR A MORSEL
FOR THE POWERS OF EVIL; GOD WILL NOT
GIVE HIS SHEEP OVER TO THE WOLFISH
JAWS OF THE PERSECUTORS. JUST WHEN
THEY ARE TUNING THEIR PIPES TO CELEBRATE
THEIR VICTORY, THEY SHALL BE MADE TO
LAUGH ON THE OTHER SIDE OF THEIR MOUTHS.
.... LITTLE DO THEY DREAM OF THE END
WHICH WILL BE PUT TO THEIR SCHEMING.
THEIR BIRDS ALL BE FLOWN, AND THEY
THEMSELVES SHALL BE IN THE TRAP!
C.H. SPURGEON -

BUT LET ALL THOSE WHO PUT
THEIR TRUST IN THEE
REJOICE:
LET THEM EVER SHOUT FOR
JOY, BECAUSE THOU
DEFENDEST THEM.
PSALM 5:11

47

Psalm 36

HOW EXCELLENT IS THY LOVING KINDNESS, O GOD! THEREFORE THE CHILDREN OF MEN PUT THEIR TRUST UNDER THE SHADOW OF THY WINGS. V.7

EVERY CHILD OF GOD LOOKS TOWARDS THE INNER SANCTUARY AND THE MERCY-SEAT, YET ALL DO NOT DWELL IN THE MOST HOLY PLACE. THOSE WHO THROUGH RICH GRACE OBTAIN UNUSUAL AND CONTINUOUS COMMUNION WITH GOD BECOME POSSESSORS OF RARE AND SPECIAL BENEFITS, WHICH ARE MISSED BY THOSE WHO FOLLOW AFAR OFF, AND GRIEVE THE HOLY SPIRIT.

SITTING DOWN IN THE AUGUST PRESENCE-CHAMBER WHERE SHINES THE MYSTIC LIGHT OF THE SHEKINAH, THEY KNOW WHAT IT IS TO BE RAISED UP, AND TO BE MADE TO SIT TOGETHER WITH CHRIST IN THE HEAVENLIES.
—C.H. SPURGEON

PSALM 37

AND THE ANGEL WHICH I SAW STAND UPON THE SEA AND UPON THE EARTH LIFTED UP HIS HAND TO HEAVEN, AND SWARE BY HIM THAT LIVETH FOR EVER AND EVER, WHO CREATED HEAVEN, AND THE THINGS THAT THEREIN ARE, AND THE EARTH, AND THE THINGS THAT THEREIN ARE, AND THE SEA, AND THE THINGS WHICH ARE THEREIN, THAT THERE SHOULD BE TIME NO LONGER: BUT IN THE DAYS OF THE VOICE OF THE SEVENTH ANGEL, WHEN HE SHALL BEGIN TO SOUND, THE MYSTERY OF GOD SHOULD BE FINISHED, AS HE HATH DECLARED TO HIS SERVANTS THE PROPHETS.

Rev 10:5-7

FOR EVIL DOERS SHALL BE CUT OFF: BUT THOSE THAT WAIT UPON THE LORD, THEY SHALL INHERIT THE EARTH.
FOR YET A LITTLE WHILE, AND THE WICKED SHALL NOT BE: YEA, THOU SHALT DILIGENTLY CONSIDER HIS PLACE, AND IT SHALL NOT BE!   PSALM 37: 9,10

BUT THE SALVATION OF THE RIGHTEOUS IS OF THE LORD: HE IS THEIR STRENGTH IN THE TIME OF TROUBLE. AND THE LORD WILL HELP THEM, AND DELIVER THEM: HE SHALL DELIVER THEM FROM THE WICKED, AND SAVE THEM .....BECAUSE THEY TRUST HIM!   PSALM 37: 39,40

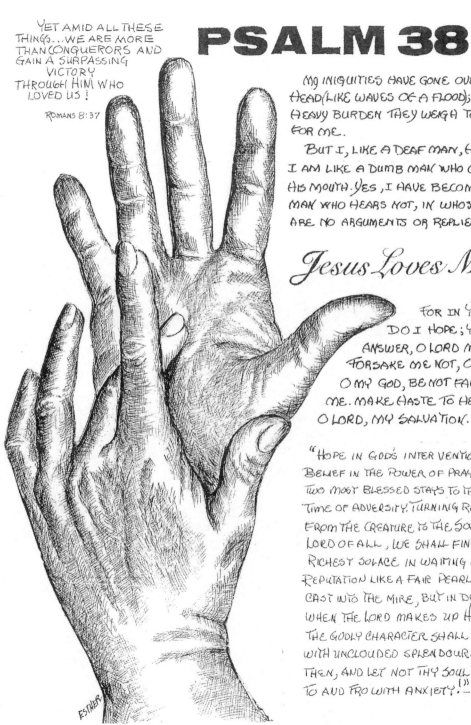

YET AMID ALL THESE
THINGS... WE ARE MORE
THAN CONQUERORS AND
GAIN A SURPASSING
VICTORY
THROUGH HIM WHO
LOVED US !

ROMANS 8:37

PSALM 38

MY INIQUITIES HAVE GONE OVER MY
HEAD (LIKE WAVES OF A FLOOD); AS A
HEAVY BURDEN THEY WEIGH TOO MUCH
FOR ME.   V. 4
    BUT I, LIKE A DEAF MAN, HEAR NOT;
I AM LIKE A DUMB MAN WHO OPENS NOT
HIS MOUTH. YES, I HAVE BECOME LIKE A
MAN WHO HEARS NOT, IN WHOSE MOUTH
ARE NO ARGUMENTS OR REPLIES. VV 13, 14

Jesus Loves Me !

        FOR IN YOU, O LORD,
     DO I HOPE; YOU WILL
        ANSWER, O LORD MY GOD.
     FORSAKE ME NOT, O LORD;
     O MY GOD, BE NOT FAR FROM
     ME. MAKE HASTE TO HELP ME,
     O LORD, MY SALVATION. VV. 15, 21, 22

"HOPE IN GOD'S INTERVENTION, AND
BELIEF IN THE POWER OF PRAYER, ARE
TWO MOST BLESSED STAYS TO THE SOUL IN
TIME OF ADVERSITY. TURNING RIGHT AWAY
FROM THE CREATURE TO THE SOVEREIGN
LORD OF ALL, WE SHALL FIND THE
RICHEST SOLACE IN WAITING UPON HIM.
REPUTATION LIKE A FAIR PEARL MAY BE
CAST INTO THE MIRE, BUT IN DUE TIME,
WHEN THE LORD MAKES UP HIS JEWELS,
THE GODLY CHARACTER SHALL SHINE
WITH UNCLOUDED SPLENDOUR... REST
THEN, AND LET NOT THY SOUL BE TOSSED
TO AND FRO WITH ANXIETY." — C.H. SPURGEON

ESTHER

PSALM 39

Lord, make me to know mine end, and the measure of my days, what it is; that I may know how frail I am. Behold, thou hast made my days as an hand breadth; and mine age is as nothing before thee: verily every man at his best state is altogether vanity. Selah. vv 4,5

AT FIRST HER MOTHER EARTH SHE HOLDETH DEAR,

    AND DOTH EMBRACE THE WORLD AND WORLDLY THINGS;

SHE FLIES CLOSE BY THE GROUND AND HOVERS HERE

    AND MOUNTS NOT UP WITH HER CELESTIAL WINGS.

YET UNDER HEAVEN SHE CANNOT LIGHT ON OUGHT

    THAT WITH HER HEAVENLY NATURE DOTH AGREE;

SHE CANNOT REST, SHE CANNOT FIX HER THOUGHT,

    SHE CANNOT IN THIS WORLD CONTENTED BE.

THEN AS A BEE WHICH AMONG WEEDS DOTH FALL,

    WHICH SEEM SWEET FLOWERS WITH LUSTER FRESH AND GAY

SHE LIGHTS ON THAT, AND THIS, AND TASTETH ALL,

    BUT PLEASED WITH NONE, DOTH RISE, AND SOAR AWAY.

SO WHEN THE SOUL FINDS HERE NO TRUE CONTENT,

    AND LIKE NOAH'S DOVE, CAN NO SURE FOOTING TAKE,

SHE DOTH RETURN FROM WHENCE SHE FIRST WAS SENT,

    .....AND FLIES TO HIM, THAT FIRST HER WINGS DID MAKE!

               — SIR JOHN DAVIES
            THE TREASURY OF DAVID

PSALM 40

OUT OF THE MIRE INTO THE CHOIR!

He DREW ME UP OUT OF A HORRIBLE PIT—A PIT OF TUMULT AND OF DISTRUCTIONS —OUT OF THE MIRY CLAY (FROTH AND SLIME) AND SET MY FEET UPON A ROCK, STEADYING MY STEPS AND ESTABLISHING MY GOINGS.

AND He HAS PUT A NEW SONG IN MY MOUTH — A SONG OF PRAISE TO GOD!

v.v. 2, 3

I was sinking deep in sin, far from the peaceful shore, very deeply stained with sin sinking to rise no more; But The Master of the sea heard my despairing cry, From the waters lifted me — Now safe am I! Love lifted me! Love lifted me! When nothing else could help — Love lifted me!

— James Rowe

DAVID'S MUD SLIDE WAS A MORAL ONE. "He HEARD ME! He HELPED ME!" THAT WAS DAVID'S TESTIMONY. UP FROM OUT OF THE MIRY CLAY! SAFE ON THE ROCK! NOW TO SING FOREVER THE PRAISE OF GOD!

AS A.P. GIBBS USED TO PUT IT; "OUT OF THE MIRE, INTO THE CHOIR!"

—JOHN PHILLIPS

THE FAITHFULNESS OF GOD IN TIMES OF EXTREMITY

I SAID, LORD, BE MERCIFUL UNTO ME; HEAL MY SOUL; FOR I HAVE SINNED AGAINST THEE.

MINE ENEMIES SPEAK EVIL OF ME, WHEN SHALL HE DIE, AND HIS NAME PERISH? BUT THOU, O LORD, BE MERCIFUL UNTO ME, AND RAISE ME UP, THAT I MAY REQUITE THEM.

BY THIS I KNOW THAT THOU FAVOREST ME — BECAUSE MINE ENEMY DOTH NOT TRIUMPH OVER ME!

PSALM 41: 4, 5, 10, 11

We are troubled on every side, yet not distressed; we are perplexed, but not in despair; persecuted, but not forsaken; cast down, but not destroyed; always bearing about in the body the dying of the Lord Jesus, that the life also of Jesus might be made manifest in our body.
2 Corinthians 4:8-10

THE FEEBLEST SAINT SHALL WIN THE DAY,
THOUGH DEATH AND HELL OBSTRUCT HIS WAY.
— C.H. SPURGEON

PSALM 41

Safe am I,
Safe am I, in the
hollow of God's hand.
Sheltered o'er, sheltered o'er,
In His love forevermore. No ill can
harm me, no foe alarm me, for He
keeps both day and night.
Safe am I, safe am I, in the hollow of God's hand.

Book Two

Psalm 42-72

PSALM 42

WHY ART THOU CAST DOWN O MY SOUL? AND WHY ART THOU DISQUIETED IN ME? HOPE THOU IN GOD! FOR I SHALL YET PRAISE HIM FOR THE HELP OF HIS COUNTENANCE.

V. 5

WHY AM I AGITATED LIKE A TROUBLED SEA, AND WHY DO MY THOUGHTS MAKE A NOISE LIKE A TUMULTUOUS MULTITUDE? THE CAUSES ARE NOT ENOUGH TO JUSTIFY SUCH YIELDING TO DESPONDENCY. UP MY HEART! WHAT AILETH THEE? "HOPE THOU IN GOD." THIS IS THE GRACE THAT SWIMS, THOUGH THE WAVES ROAR AND BE TROUBLED.

GOD IS UNCHANGEABLE, AND THEREFORE HIS GRACE IS THE GROUND FOR UNSHAKEN HOPE. IF EVERYTHING BE DARK, YET THE DAY WILL COME, AND MEANWHILE HOPE CARRIES STARS IN HER EYES; HER LAMPS ARE NOT DEPENDENT UPON OIL FROM WITHOUT — HER LIGHT IS FED BY SECRET VISITATIONS OF GOD, WHICH SUSTAIN THE SPIRIT.

"FOR I SHALL YET PRAISE HIM." YET WILL MY SIGHS GIVE PLACE TO SONGS, MY MOURNFUL DITTIES SHALL BE EXCHANGED FOR TRIUMPHAL PAEANS. A LOSS OF THE PRESENT SENSE OF GOD'S LOVE IS NOT A LOSS OF THAT LOVE ITSELF; THE JEWEL IS THERE, THOUGH IT GLEAMS NOT IN OUR BREAST; HOPE KNOWS HER TITLE GOOD WHEN SHE CANNOT READ IT CLEAR; SHE EXPECTS THE PROMISED BOON THOUGH PRESENT PROVIDENCE STANDS BEFORE HER WITH EMPTY HANDS.

— C.H. SPURGEON

PSALM 43

O SEND OUT THY LIGHT AND THY TRUTH: LET THEM LEAD ME; LET THEM BRING ME UNTO THY HOLY HILL, AND TO THY TABERNACLES. THEN WILL I GO UNTO THE ALTAR OF GOD ...UNTO GOD MY EXCEEDING JOY! YEA UPON THE HARP WILL I PRAISE THEE, O GOD MY GOD. VV 3,4

What a word of triumph! Now the psalmist understands what God has been doing in his life. Step by step God has been driving him to the ultimate refuge of any believer in a time of testing: the Word of God......God's word is light and truth, and the psalmist cries out for the light of God's promises to shine forth and strengthen his heart. What a revelation this is! For each of us as believers, there comes a time when we discover for ourselves that the God of the universe is our own personal God, our intimate Friend, and our Refuge......That's the power of God's word to send forth light and truth into lives filled with darkness. That's the power of the Bible to transform a wretched sinner into a godly saint. That's the power of God's Word to enter our gloom and depression and lift us up to the holy mountain where God dwells. That's what the psalmist is saying. When you can't shake the blues and you suffer from a depression that nothing relieves, then there's only one thing to do: Rest upon God's Word. Let Him send forth His light and truth into your soul. Listen to the sweet and soothing words of the Bible, and especially the Psalms. Let those word guide you, lift your spirit, and heal your heart.   Ray C. Stedman

THE WORD OF GOD

HOPE

Psalm 44

YOU ARE MY KING, O GOD;
COMMAND VICTORIES AND DELIVERANCE
FOR JACOB.
v.4

WHAT A BATTLE-SHOUT THIS IS! WHENEVER TEMPTATION IS NEAR; WHEN THE
FOE SEEMS ABOUT TO TAKE THE CITADEL BY ASSAULT; WHEN HEART AND FLESH QUAIL
BEFORE THE NOISE OF BATTLE ___ THEN TO LOOK UP TO THE LIVING CHRIST, AND SAY,
THOU ART MY KING, O SON OF GOD: COMMAND VICTORY!

THERE IS NO DEVIL IN HELL THAT WOULD NOT FLEE BEFORE THAT CRY
OF THE TEMPTED AND TRIED BELIEVER ___ AND GOD COULD NOT BE
NEGLECTFUL OF SUCH AN APPEAL!
— F.B. MEYER

PSALM 45

HEARKEN, O DAUGHTER, AND CONSIDER, AND INCLINE THINE EAR; FORGET ALSO THINE OWN PEOPLE, AND THY FATHER'S HOUSE. SO SHALL THE KING GREATLY DESIRE THY BEAUTY; FOR HE IS THY LORD — AND WORSHIP THOU HIM...THE KING'S DAUGHTER IS ALL GLORIOUS WITHIN. HER CLOTHING IS OF WROUGHT GOLD. SHE SHALL BE BROUGHT UNTO THE KING IN RAIMENT OF NEEDLEWORK.   VV 10, 11, 13, 14

RAIMENT OF NEEDLEWORK! IN THE BIBLE CLOTHING IS USED SYMBOLICALLY. TO DESCRIBE RIGHTEOUSNESS AND CHARACTER. THIS IS ESPECIALLY TRUE OF LINEN. THERE IS WHITE LINEN, THE RIGHTEOSNESS OF CHRIST, AND WHITE LINEN, THE RIGHTEOUSNESS OF SAINTS. THERE IS THE RIGHTEOUSNESS THAT IS BROUGHT TO US, WHEN WE COME TO CHRIST HE ARRAYS US IN THE WEDDING GARMENT OF SALVATION, TAKES AWAY THAT RUIN OF RAGS WE WORE IN OUR UNCONVERTED DAYS, AND MAKES US FIT FOR THE HIGH HALLS OF HEAVEN....BUT THERE IS MORE TO IT THAN THAT; THERE IS THE RIGHTEOUSNESS THAT IS WROUGHT IN US. THE HOLY SPIRIT GOES TO WORK ON US TO MAKE US LIKE JESUS — THAT'S THE RAIMENT OF NEEDLEWORK, THE EMBROIDERY SO TO SPEAK, THE BEAUTIFICATION OF OUR LIVES AND CHARACTERS BY THE WORKING OF THE SPIRIT OF GOD IN US.

— JOHN PHILLIPS

THE WEDDING
...AT LAST!

PSALM 46

GOD IS OUR REFUGE AND STRENGTH, A VERY PRESENT HELP IN TROUBLE. THEREFORE WILL NOT WE FEAR, THOUGH THE EARTH BE REMOVED, AND THOUGH THE MOUNTAINS BE CARRIED INTO THE MIDST OF THE SEA; THOUGH THE WATERS THEREOF ROAR AND BE TROUBLED, THOUGH THE MOUNTAINS SHAKE WITH THE SWELLING THEREOF. SELAH! ~ V 1-3

WHEN ALL THINGS ARE EXCITED TO FURY, AND REVEAL THEIR UTMOST POWER TO DISTURB, FAITH SMILES SERENELY. SHE IS NOT AFRAID OF NOISE, NOT EVEN REAL FORCE, SHE KNOWS THAT THE LORD STILLETH THE RAGING SEA, AND HOLDETH THE WAVES IN THE HOLLOW OF HIS HAND... ALPS AND ANDES MAY TREMBLE, BUT FAITH RESTS ON A FIRMER BASIS, AND IS NOT MOVED BY SWELLING SEAS. EVIL MAY FERMENT, WRATH MAY BOIL, AND PRIDE MAY FOAM, BUT THE BRAVE HEART OF HOLY CONFIDENCE TREMBLES NOT!

—C.H. SPURGEON

PSALM 47

Sing praises to God, sing praises; sing praises unto our King, sing praises.

For God is the King of all the earth, sing ye praises with understanding.

God reigneth over the heathen; God sitteth upon the throne of His holiness.

The princes of the peoples are gathered together, even the people of the God of Abraham; for the shields of the earth belong unto God. He is greatly exalted!

v.v 6-9

What jubilation is here, when five times the whole earth is called upon to sing to God! He is worthy, He is Creator, He is goodness itself, sing praises, keep on with the glad work. Never let the music pause. He never ceases to be good, let us never cease to be grateful. Strange that we should need so much urging to attend to so heavenly an exercise... Let Him have all our praise; no one ought to have a particle of it. Jesus shall have it all. Let His sovereignty be the fount of gladness. It is a sublime attribute, but full of bliss to the faithful.

Let our homage be paid not in groans but in songs. He asks not slaves to grace His throne; He is no despot; singing is fit homage for a monarch so blessed and gracious. Let all hearts that own His sceptre sing and sing on forever, for there is everlasting reason for thanksgiving while we dwell under the shadow of such a throne!

— C.H. SPURGEON

PSALM 48

GREAT IS THE LORD, AND GREATLY TO BE PRAISED IN THE CITY OF OUR GOD; IN THE MOUNTAIN OF HIS HOLINESS. V1.

ACCORDING TO THY NAME, O GOD, SO IS THY PRAISE UNTO THE ENDS OF THE EARTH; THY RIGHT HAND IS FULL OF RIGHTEOUSNESS. V10

WHEN CHRIST SHALL COME WITH SHOUT OF ACCLAMATION,
AND TAKE ME HOME, WHAT JOY SHALL FILL MY HEART!
THEN I SHALL BOW IN HUMBLE ADORATION
AND THERE PROCLAIM, MY GOD, HOW GREAT
THOU ART!
THEN SINGS MY SOUL, MY SAVIOR GOD, TO THEE;
HOW GREAT THOU ART, HOW GREAT THOU ART!
THEN SINGS MY SOUL, MY SAVIOR GOD, TO THEE;
HOW GREAT THOU ART, HOW GREAT THOU ART!
— STUART K. HINE. 1899

AS IN A SHELL WE LISTEN TO THE MURMURS OF THE SEA, SO IN THE CONVOLUTIONS OF CREATION WE HEAR THE PRAISES OF GOD. ...THY SCEPTRE AND THY SWORD, THY GOVERNMENT AND THY VENGEANCE, ARE ALTOGETHER JUST.

THE RIGHTEOUS ACTS OF THE LORD ARE LEGITIMATE SUBJECTS FOR JOYFUL PRAISE. HOWEVER IT MAY APPEAR ON EARTH, YET IN HEAVEN THE ETERNAL RUIN OF THE WICKED WILL BE THE THEME OF ADORING SONG.
"HALLELUJAH! SALVATION, AND GLORY,
AND HONOR, AND POWER, UNTO THE
LORD, OUR GOD!" REV. 19:1
— C.H. SPURGEON

FOR THIS GOD IS OUR GOD FOREVER AND EVER; HE WILL BE OUR GUIDE EVEN UNTO DEATH.
PSALM 48:14

OH, SWEET WORD "EVER". ALL THE ARITHMETICAL FIGURES OF DAYS, AND MONTHS AND YEARS AND AGES ARE NOTHING TO THIS INFINITE CIPHER "EVER"; YEA, OUR MILLIONS AND MILLIONS OF MILLIONS ARE LESS THAN DROPS TO THIS OCEAN....
"EVER"! — GEORGE SWINNOCK

62

PSALM 49 The Ransom

THEY THAT TRUST IN THEIR WEALTH AND BOAST THEMSELVES IN THE MULTITUDE OF THEIR RICHES; NONE OF THEM CAN BY ANY MEANS REDEEM HIS BROTHER NOR GIVE TO GOD A RANSOM FOR HIM.

FOR THE REDEMPTION OF THEIR SOUL IS PRECIOUS AND IT CEASETH FOREVER. BUT GOD WILL REDEEM MY SOUL FROM THE POWER OF THE GRAVE; FOR HE SHALL RECEIVE ME. VV. 6-8, 15

FOR AS MUCH AS YE KNOW THAT YE WERE NOT REDEEMED WITH CORRUPTIBLE THINGS, AS SILVER AND GOLD, FROM YOUR VAIN CONVERSATION RECEIVED BY TRADITION FROM YOUR FATHERS—BUT WITH THE PRECIOUS BLOOD OF CHRIST, AS A LAMB WITHOUT BLEMISH AND WITHOUT SPOT.
1 PETER 1:18-19

EVEN AS THE SON OF MAN CAME NOT TO BE MINISTERED UNTO–BUT TO MINISTER AND GIVE HIS LIFE A RANSOM FOR MANY. MATT. 20:28

"BLESSED
IS THE MAN WHO HAS REALIZED HIS UTTER HELPLESSNESS, AND WHO HAS PUT HIS WHOLE TRUST IN GOD. IF A MAN HAS REALIZED THIS THERE WILL ENTER INTO HIS LIFE TWO THINGS WHICH ARE OPPOSITE SIDES OF THE SAME THING...HE WILL BECOME COMPLETELY DETACHED FROM THE THINGS, FOR HE WILL KNOW THAT THINGS HAVE NOT GOT IT IN THEM TO BRING HAPPINESS OR SECURITY; AND HE WILL BECOME COMPLETELY ATTACTED TO GOD, FOR HE WILL KNOW THAT GOD ALONE CAN BRING HIM HELP, AND THE HOPE, AND STRENGTH.
THE MAN WHO IS POOR IN SPIRIT IS THE MAN WHO HAS REALIZED THAT THINGS MEAN NOTHING, AND THAT GOD MEANS EVERYTHING!"

--WILLIAM BARCLAY

PSALM 50

OFFER UNTO GOD THANKSGIVING; AND PAY THY VOWS UNTO THE MOST HIGH; AND CALL UPON ME IN THE DAY OF TROUBLE — I WILL DELIVER THEE, AND THOU SHALT GLORIFY ME.   VV 14,15

WHOSO OFFERETH PRAISE GLORIFIES ME: AND TO HIM THAT ORDERETH HIS CONVERSATION ARIGHT WILL I SHOW THE SALVATION OF GOD.   V 23

Have you ever asked yourself, "Why do the Scriptures stress thanksgiving so much?" "Give thanks in all circumstances," says the apostle Paul, "for this is God's will for you in Christ Jesus." (1 Thess. 5:18) You say "thank you: when someone has given you something you didn't already have. Thanksgiving is the proper expression of genuine Christianity because Christianity, at its very essence, is a lifestyle of continually receiving something from God (grace, forgiveness, and salvation) that we are incapable of supplying by ourselves. If you have not received anything form God, you can't be thankful, and if you aren't thankful, then you've probably never received the gift He wants to give you. God is a realist. He doesn't want phony expressions of thanksgiving. ——Ray Stedman

PSALM 51

HAVE MERCY UPON ME, O GOD, ACCORDING UNTO THE MULTITUDE OF THY TENDER MERCIES BLOT OUT MY TRANSGRESSIONS CREATE IN ME A CLEAN HEART O GOD; AND RENEW A RIGHT SPIRIT WITHIN ME. RESTORE UNTO ME THE JOY OF THY SALVATION, AND UPHOLD ME WITH THY FREE SPIRIT. THEN WILL I TEACH TRANSGRESSORS THY WAYS; AND SINNERS SHALL BE CONVERTED UNTO THEE

VV 1, 10, 12, 13

NONE BUT GOD CAN CREATE EITHER A NEW HEART OR A NEW EARTH. SALVATION IS A MARVELOUS DISPLAY OF SUPREME POWER; THE WORK IN US AS MUCH AS THAT FOR US IS WHOLLY OF OMNIPOTENCE. THE AFFECTIONS MUST BE RECTIFIED FIRST, OR ALL OUR NATURE WILL GO AMISS. THE HEART IS THE RUDDER OF THE SOUL, AND TILL THE LORD TAKE IT IN HAND WE STEER IN A FALSE AND FOUL WAY. O LORD, THOU WHO DIDST ONCE MAKE ME, BE PLEASED TO MAKE ME NEW, AND IN MY MOST SECRET PARTS RENEW ME. "RENEW A RIGHT SPIRIT WITHIN ME." IT WAS THERE ONCE, LORD, PUT IT THERE AGAIN.

"RESTORE UNTO ME THE JOY OF THY SALVATION." NONE BUT GOD CAN GIVE BACK THIS JOY; HE CAN DO IT; WE MAY ASK IT; HE WILL DO IT FOR HIS OWN GLORY AND OUR BENEFIT. THIS JOY COMES NOT FIRST, BUT FOLLOWS PARDON AND PURITY.

"AND UPHOLD ME WITH THY FREE SPIRIT." THAT ROYAL SPIRIT, WHOSE HOLINESS IS TRUE DIGNITY, IS ABLE TO MAKE US WALK AS KINGS AND PRIESTS, IN ALL THE UPRIGHTNESS OF HOLINESS; AND HE WILL DO SO IF WE SEEK HIS GRACIOUS UPHOLDING!
-C.H. SPURGEON

PSALM 52

WHY BOASTEST THOU THYSELF IN MISCHIEF,
O MIGHTY MAN? THE GOODNESS OF GOD
ENDURETH CONTINUALLY... GOD SHALL
LIKEWISE DESTROY THEE FOREVER; HE
SHALL TAKE THEE AWAY, AND PLUCK THEE
OUT OF THE LAND OF THE LIVING. SELAH
... BUT I AM LIKE A GREEN OLIVE TREE
IN THE HOUSE OF GOD; I TRUST IN THE
MERCY OF GOD FOREVER AND EVER.

V.V. 1, 5, 8

"BUT I", HUNTED AND PERSECUTED THOUGH
I AM, "AM LIKE A GREEN OLIVE TREE." I AM NOT
PLUCKED UP OR DESTROYED, BUT AM LIKE A
FLOURISHING OLIVE, WHICH OUT OF THE ROCK
DRAWS OIL, AND AMID THE DROUGHT STILL LIVES
AND GROWS, "IN THE HOUSE OF GOD."
    HE WAS ONE OF THE DIVINE FAMILY, AND
COULD NOT BE EXPELLED FROM IT, HIS PLACE WAS
NEAR HIS GOD, AND THERE WAS HE SAFE AND
HAPPY DESPITE ALL HIS FOES.
    HE WAS BEARING FRUIT, AND WOULD CONTINUE
TO DO SO WHEN ALL HIS PROUD ENEMIES WERE
WITHERED LIKE BRANCHES LOPPED FROM THE TREE.

—C.H. SPURGEON

THERE ARE THREE WAYS OF BECOMING LIKE A GREEN OLIVE TREE:
1. TRUST IN THE MERCY OF GOD: TO TRUST WHEN THE LIGHT HAS BURNT TO ITS SOCKET, IN THE
HOUSE OF LIFE, AND THE HEART IS AS LONELY AS JOB'S AMID THE WRECK OF HIS HOME. TO KNOW
THAT ALL IS WELL, THAT SEEMS MOST ILL. THIS KEEPS THE HEART FROM WITHERING.
2. THANKSGIVING — THERE IS ALWAYS SOMETHING TO THANK GOD FOR.
3. WAITING ON GOD — NOT ALWAYS TALKING TO HIM OR ABOUT HIM, BUT WAITING BEFORE HIM TILL
THE STREAM RUNS CLEAR — TILL THE CREAM RISES TO THE TOP — TILL THE MISTS PART, AND THE
SOUL REGAINS ITS EQUILIBRIUM — THIS KEEPS THE SOUL CALM AND QUIET. —F.B. MEYER

PSALM 53

THE FOOL HATH SAID IN HIS HEART, THERE IS NO GOD. CORRUPT ARE THEY, AND HAVE DONE ABOMINABLE INIQUITY: THERE IS NONE THAT DOETH GOOD.

GOD LOOKED DOWN FROM HEAVEN UPON THE CHILDREN OF MEN, TO SEE IF THERE WERE ANY THAT DID UNDERSTAND, THAT DID SEEK GOD. VV 1,2

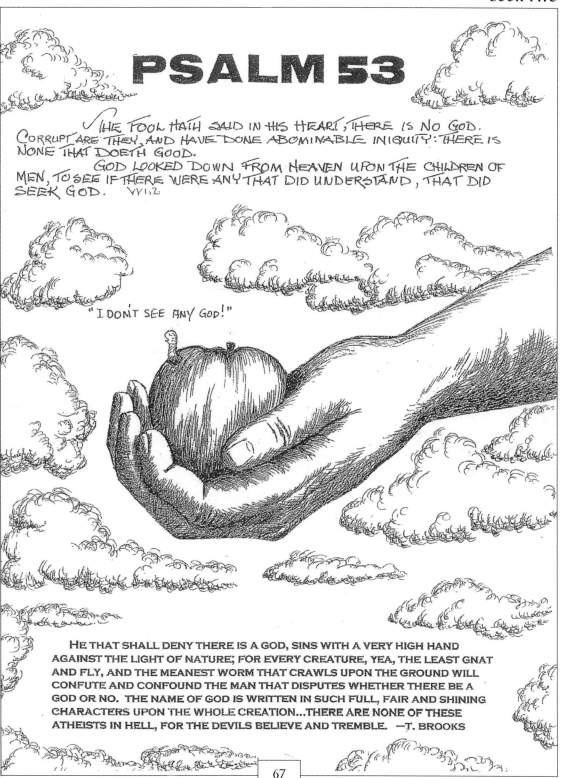

"I DON'T SEE ANY GOD!"

HE THAT SHALL DENY THERE IS A GOD, SINS WITH A VERY HIGH HAND AGAINST THE LIGHT OF NATURE; FOR EVERY CREATURE, YEA, THE LEAST GNAT AND FLY, AND THE MEANEST WORM THAT CRAWLS UPON THE GROUND WILL CONFUTE AND CONFOUND THE MAN THAT DISPUTES WHETHER THERE BE A GOD OR NO. THE NAME OF GOD IS WRITTEN IN SUCH FULL, FAIR AND SHINING CHARACTERS UPON THE WHOLE CREATION...THERE ARE NONE OF THESE ATHEISTS IN HELL, FOR THE DEVILS BELIEVE AND TREMBLE. —T. BROOKS

PSALM 54

SAVE ME, O GOD, BY THY NAME, AND JUDGE ME BY THY STRENGTH. HEAR MY PRAYER, O GOD; GIVE EAR TO THE WORDS OF MY MOUTH.
BEHOLD, GOD IS MINE HELPER!
V.V. 1, 2, 4

FOR HE HATH DELIVERED ME OUT OF ALL TROUBLE; AND MINE EYE HATH SEEN HIS DESIRE UPON MINE ENEMIES.
V.7

OH, TO REALIZE THE TREMENDOUS TRUTH, THAT WHEN WE ACCEPT GOD'S GRACIOUS INVITATION TO "COME BOLDLY TO THE THRONE OF GRACE," OUR WORDS, OUR SIGHS, OUR TEARS, ARE HEARD! EARNEST, HEART-FELT PRAYER PIERCES THROUGH THE MISTS OF CONFUSION, THE SHADOWS OF FEAR, THE DARK CLOUDS OF DESPAIR. IT SPEEDS THROUGH THE GALAXIES OF SPACE, THROUGH THE GATES OF PEARL, DOWN THE STREETS OF GOLD, PAST THE MAGNIFICENT MANSIONS, THROUGH THE THRONGS OF PRAISING SAINTS AND ANGELS, PAST THE CHERUBIM AND SERAPHIM AROUND THE THRONE, RIGHT TO THE VERY EAR OF ALMIGHTY GOD.... OUR FATHER!

WINGS!

PSALM 55

AND I SAID, OH THAT I HAD WINGS
LIKE A DOVE ! FOR THEN WOULD I FLY
AWAY AND BE AT REST.
LO, THEN WOULD I WANDER
FAR OFF, AND REMAIN IN THE
WILDERNESS.   SELAH   V 6, 7

WHEN YOU PRAY, BUT
CANNOT GET YOUR ANSWER
THROUGH;
WHEN YOU ARE DISCOURAGED,
KNOW NOT WHAT TO DO,
CEASE TO BEG AND PLEAD, BUT
HALLELUJAHS RAISE...
YOUR PETITION SHALL ASCEND ON
WINGS OF PRAISE!

RISE AND SOAR INTO THE SUNLIT RAYS,
USING BOTH THE WINGS OF PRAYER AND
PRAISE
MOUNT LIKE EAGLES, HIGHER IN THE SKY
AND YOU WILL FIND THINGS LOOK SO DIFFERENT
WHEN YOU FLY!

— UNKNOWN

WHEN PEACE LIKE A RIVER, ATTENDETH MY WAY,
WHEN SORROWS LIKE SEA BILLOWS ROLL;
WHATEVER MY LOT, THOU HAST TAUGHT ME TO SAY,
IT IS WELL... IT IS WELL WITH MY SOUL.

THOUGH SATAN SHOULD BUFFET, THO' TRIALS SHOULD COME,
LET THIS BLEST ASSURANCE CONTROL,
THAT CHRIST HAS REGARDED MY HELPLESS ESTATE,
AND HATH SHED HIS OWN BLOOD FOR MY SOUL!

AND, LORD, HASTE THE DAY WHEN THE FAITH SHALL BE SIGHT, THE CLOUDS BE ROLLED BACK
AS A SCROLL, THE TRUMP SHALL RESOUND AND THE LORD SHALL DESCEND, EVEN SO...
IT IS WELL WITH MY SOUL... IT IS WELL, IT IS WELL WITH MY SOUL... IT IS WELL...

— HORATIO G. SPAFFORD

PSALM 56

"...AND A BOOK OF REMEMBRANCE WAS WRITTEN BEFORE HIM FOR THEM THAT FEARED THE LORD, AND THAT THOUGHT UPON HIS NAME."
MALACHI 3:16

THOU TELLEST MY WANDERINGS: PUT THOU MY TEARS INTO THY BOTTLE...ARE THEY NOT IN THY BOOK? V.8

"FOR THE LAMB WHICH IS IN THE MIDST OF THE THRONE SHALL FEED THEM, AND SHALL LEAD THEM UNTO LIVING FOUNTAINS OF WATERS...AND GOD SHALL WIPE AWAY ALL TEARS FROM THEIR EYES."
REV. 7:17

PSALM 57

YEA, IN THE SHADOW OF THY WINGS WILL I MAKE MY REFUGE UNTIL THESE CALAMITIES BE OVERPAST.
V-1

AS A LITTLE BIRD FINDS AMPLE SHELTER BENEATH THE PARENTAL WING, EVEN SO WOULD THE FUGITIVE PLACE HIMSELF BENEATH THE SECURE PROTECTION OF THE DIVINE POWER... WHEN WE CANNOT SEE THE SUNSHINE OF GOD'S FACE, IT IS BLESSED TO COWER DOWN BENEATH THE SHADOW OF HIS WINGS. ...

.... EVIL WILL PASS AWAY, AND THE ETERNAL WING WILL ABIDE OVER US TILL THEN.

BLESSED BE GOD, OUR CALAMITIES ARE MATTERS OF TIME, BUT OUR SAFETY IS A MATTER OF ETERNITY!
— C. H. SPURGEON

HE THAT DWELLETH IN THE SECRET PLACE OF THE MOST HIGH SHALL ABIDE UNDER THE SHADOW OF THE ALMIGHTY. I WILL SAY OF THE LORD, HE IS MY REFUGE AND MY FORTRESS: MY GOD; IN HIM WILL I TRUST.
SURELY HE SHALL DELIVER THEE FROM THE SNARE OF THE FOWLER, AND FROM THE NOISOME PESTILENCE.
HE SHALL COVER THEE WITH HIS FEATHERS, AND UNDER HIS WINGS SHALT THOU TRUST.
PSALM 91:1-4

"JESUS LOVER OF MY SOUL LET ME TO THY BOSOM FLY, WHILE THE NEARER WATERS ROLL WHILE THE TEMPEST STILL IS HIGH HIDE ME, O MY SAVIOUR, HIDE TILL THE STORM OF LIFE IS PAST"

JUSTICE!

Verily there is a reward for the righteous......
Verily He is a God that judgeth in the earth. v 11

*But with righteousness shall he judge the poor and reprove with equity
for the meek of the earth; and He shall smith the earth with the rod of
His mouth, and with the breath of his lips shall He slay the wicked.
The wolf also shall dwell with the lamb and the leopard shall lie down
with the kid; and the calf and the young lion and the fatling
together...and a little child shall lead them.*

Isaiah 11: 4, 6

*"Two things will come out after all---
There is a God and there is a reward
for the righteous....Meanwhile faith's
foreseeing eye discerns the truth even
now and is glad!"
---Charles H. Spurgeon*

PSALM 58

PSALM 59

DELIVER ME FROM MINE ENEMIES, O MY GOD; DEFEND ME FROM THEM THAT RISE UP AGAINST ME. V.1

"SAFE AM I, SAFE AM I, IN THE HOLLOW OF GOD'S HAND
SHELTERED OER, SHELTERED OER, IN HIS LOVE FOREVERMORE,
NO ILL CAN HARM ME, NO FOE ALARM ME, FOR HE KEEPS
BOTH DAY AND NIGHT, SAFE AM I, SAFE AM I, IN THE
HOLLOW OF GOD'S HAND!"

BUT I WILL SING OF THY POWER; YEA, I WILL SING ALOUD OF THY MERCY IN THE MORNING: FOR THOU HAST BEEN MY DEFENCE AND REFUGE IN THE DAY OF MY TROUBLE. VV 16, 17

"WHAT A BLESSED MORNING WILL SOON BREAK FOR THE RIGHTEOUS, AND WHAT A SONG WILL BE THEIRS! TUNE YOUR HARPS EVEN NOW, FOR THE SIGNAL TO COMMENCE THE ETERNAL MUSIC WILL SOON BE GIVEN.

... THE GREATER OUR PRESENT TRIALS THE LOUDER WILL OUR FUTURE SONGS BE, AND THE MORE INTENSE OUR JOYFUL GRATITUDE."

"AND WHEN IT SEEMS NO CHANCE NOR CHANGE FROM GRIEF CAN SET ME FREE,
HOPE FINDS ITS STRENGTH IN HELPLESSNESS,
AND, PATIENT, WAITS ON THEE."
— C.H. SPURGEON

PSALM 60

BUT NOW YOU HAVE SET UP A BANNER FOR THOSE WHO FEAR AND WORSHIPFULLY REVERE YOU (TO WHICH THEY MAY FLEE FROM THE BOW), A STANDARD DISPLAYED BECAUSE OF THE TRUTH ... SELAH ... PAUSE AND CALMLY THINK OF THAT! THAT YOUR BELOVED ONES MAY BE DELIVERED, SAVE WITH YOUR RIGHT HAND AND ANSWER US. ... THROUGH GOD WE SHALL DO VALIANTLY, FOR HE IT IS WHO SHALL TREAD DOWN OUR ADVERSARIES!

V.V. 4,5,12

THE LORD HAS CALLED BACK TO HIMSELF HIS SERVANTS, AND COMMISSIONED THEM FOR HIS SERVICE, PRESENTING THEM WITH A STANDARD TO BE USED IN HIS WARS. HE GAVE THEM AN ENSIGN WHICH WOULD BE BOTH A RALLYING POINT FOR THEIR HOSTS, A PROOF THAT HE HAS SENT THEM TO FIGHT, AND A GUARANTEE OF VICTORY. THE BRAVEST MEN ARE USUALLY INTRUSTED WITH THE BANNER, AND IT IS CERTAIN THAT THOSE WHO FEAR GOD MOST HAVE LESS FEAR THAN ANY OTHERS.

THE LORD HAS GIVEN US THE STANDARD OF THE GOSPEL, LET US LIVE TO UPHOLD IT, AND IF NEEDFUL DIE TO DEFEND IT. BANNERS ARE FOR THE BREEZE, THE SUN, THE BATTLE.

TO PUBLISH THE GOSPEL IS A SACRED DUTY, TO BE ASHAMED OF IT IS A DEADLY SIN ... FOR THE TRUTHS SAKE, AND BECAUSE THE TRUE GOD IS ON OUR SIDE, LET US IN THESE MODERN DAYS OF WARFARE EMULATE THE WARRIORS OF ISRAEL, AND UNFURL OUR BANNERS TO THE BREEZE WITH CONFIDENT JOY!

— C.H. SPURGEON

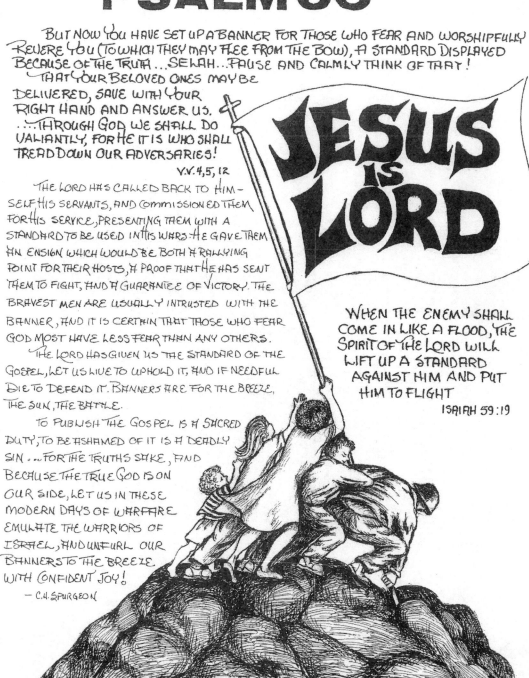

JESUS IS LORD

WHEN THE ENEMY SHALL COME IN LIKE A FLOOD, THE SPIRIT OF THE LORD WILL LIFT UP A STANDARD AGAINST HIM AND PUT HIM TO FLIGHT

ISAIAH 59:19

HEAR MY CRY OH GOD; ATTEND UNTO MY PRAYER. FROM THE END OF THE EARTH WILL I CRY UNTO THEE, WHEN MY HEART IS OVERWHELMED; LEAD ME TO THE ROCK THAT IS HIGHTER THAN I.

FOR THOU HAST BEEN A SHELTER FOR ME, AND A STRONG TOWER FROM THE ENEMY. VV. 1-3

PSALM 61

Hiding In Thee
O safe to the Rock that is higher than I my soul in it's conflicts and sorrows would fly. So sinful, so weary—Thine, Thine would I be; Thou blest "Rock of Ages," I'm hiding in Thee.

In the calm of the noon-tide, in sorrow's lone hour, in times when temptation casts o'er me it's pow'r, in the tempests of life, on it's wide, heaving sea; Thou blest "Rock of Ages," I'm hiding in Thee.

How oft in the conflict, when pressed by the foe, I have fled to my Refuge and breathed out my woe. How often, when trials like sea billows roll, have I hidden in Thee, O Thou Rock of my soul.

Hiding in Thee, Thou blest "Rock of Ages", I'm hiding in Thee.
WM Cushing

PSALM 62

MY SOUL, WAIT THOU ONLY UPON GOD; FOR MY EXPECTATION IS FROM HIM.

HE ONLY IS MY ROCK AND MY SALVATION; HE IS MY DEFENCE: I SHALL NOT BE MOVED.

IN GOD IS MY SALVATION AND MY GLORY; THE ROCK OF MY STRENGTH AND MY REFUGE, IS IN GOD.   VV. 5-7

No eloquence in all the world is half so full of meaning as the patient silence of a child of God. It is an eminent work of grace to bring down the will and subdue the affections to such a degree, that the whole mind lies before the Lord like a sea beneath the wind, ready to be moved by every breath of His mouth, but free from all power to be moved by anything other than the divine will! C. H. Spurgeon

PSALM 63

O'GOD, THOU ART MY GOD; EARLY WILL I SEEK THEE: MY SOUL THIRSTETH FOR THEE. MY FLESH LONGETH FOR THEE IN A DRY AND THIRSTY LAND WHERE NO WATER IS.

MY SOUL SHALL BE SATISFIED WITH MARROW AND FATNESS; AND MY MOUTH SHALL PRAISE THEE WITH JOYFUL LIPS: BECAUSE THOU HAST BEEN MY HELP—THEREFORE IN THE SHADOW OF THY WINGS WILL I REJOICE!

MY SOUL FOLLOWETH HARD AFTER THEE: THY RIGHT HAND UPHOLDETH ME!   VV 1, 5, 7, 8

"THEREFORE IN THE SHADOW OF THY WINGS WILL I REJOICE." UNDER THE EAGLE WINGS OF JEHOVAH WE HIDE FROM ALL FEAR, AND WE DO THIS NATURALLY AND AT ONCE, BECAUSE WE HAVE AFORETIME TRIED AND PROVED BOTH HIS LOVE AND HIS POWER. WE ARE NOT ONLY SAFE, BUT HAPPY IN GOD; WE REJOICE AS WELL AS REPOSE!

AS A BIRD SHELTERED IN THE RICH FOLIAGE FROM THE HEAT OF THE SUN, SINGS ITS MERRY NOTES; SO WE CELEBRATE OUR SONGS OF PRAISE FROM THE SHADOW OF THE WINGS OF GOD.

— C.H. SPURGEON

PSALM 64

HEAR MY VOICE, O GOD, IN MY PRAYER; PRESERVE MY LIFE FROM FEAR OF THE ENEMY.

Hide me from the secret counsel of the wicked:
from the insurrection of the workers of iniquity;
who whet their tongue like a sword, and bend their bows
to shoot their arrows, even bitter words;
that they may shoot in secret at the perfect;
but God shall shoot at them with an arrow:
suddenly shall they be wounded! Verses 1-4, 7

The righteous shall be glad in the Lord, and shall trust in him; and all the upright in heart shall glory! v 10

Walk in the light as He is in the light; cultivate the habit of considering what has been given, rather than what has been withheld, and you will find that he will make you glad in proportion to the days in which you have seen evil. The sad heart tires in a mile ---the glad heart mounts up with wings as eagles. F.B MEYER

Psalm 65

BLESSED IS THE MAN WHOM THOU CHOOSEST, AND CAUSEST TO APPROACH UNTO THEE, THAT HE MAY DWELL IN THY COURTS; HE SHALL BE SATISFIED WITH THE GOODNESS OF THY HOUSE, EVEN OF THY HOLY TEMPLE. V.4

WHICH BY HIS STRENGTH SETTETH FAST THE MOUNTAINS; BEING GIRDED WITH POWER! V.6

HALLELUJAH! THE ONE WHO FORMED THE MOUNTAINS HOLDS MY HAND!

... FIRST, WE ARE CHOSEN BY GOD, ACCORDING TO THE GOOD PLEASURE OF HIS WILL, AND THIS ALONE IS BLESSEDNESS. THEN, SINCE WE CANNOT AND WILL NOT COME TO GOD OF OURSELVES, HE WORKS GRACIOUSLY IN US, AND ATTRACTS US POWERFULLY; HE SUBDUES OUR UNWILLINGNESS, AND REMOVES OUR INABILITY BY THE ALMIGHTY WORKINGS OF HIS TRANSFORMING GRACE. THIS ALSO IS NO SLIGHT BLESSEDNESS. FURTHERMORE, WE, BY HIS DIVINE DRAWINGS ARE MADE NIGH BY THE BLOOD OF HIS SON, AND BROUGHT NEAR BY HIS SPIRIT, INTO INTIMATE FELLOWSHIP; SO THAT WE HAVE ACCESS WITH BOLDNESS, AND ARE NO LONGER AS THOSE WHO ARE AFAR OFF BY WICKED WORKS. TO CROWN ALL, WE APPROACH AS CHOSEN AND ACCEPTED ONES, TO BECOME DWELLERS IN THE DIVINE HOUSEHOLD: THIS IS HEAPED UP BLESSEDNESS, VAST BEYOND CONCEPTION. BUT DWELLING IN THE HOUSE WE ARE TREATED AS SONS!

NO MORE A STRANGER OR A GUEST, BUT LIKE A CHILD AT HOME."

—C.H. SPURGEON

PSALM 66

SILVER IS TRIED BY FIRE, AND THE HEART BY PAIN. BUT IN THE FIRE THOU SHALT NOT BE BURNED; ONLY THY DROSS REMOVED. THE SMELL OF BURNING SHALL NOT PASS UPON THEE, FOR THE FORM OF THE SON OF GOD SHALL BE AT THY SIDE.

THE MAIN END OF LIFE IS NOT TO DO—BUT TO BECOME. FOR THIS WE ARE BEING MOLDED AND DISCIPLINED EACH HOUR. YOU CANNOT UNDERSTAND WHY YEAR AFTER YEAR THE STERN ORDEAL GOES ON; YOU THINK THE TIME IS WASTED; YOU ARE DOING NOTHING. YES, BUT YOU ARE SITUATED IN THE SET OF CIRCUMSTANCES THAT GIVES YOU THE BEST OPPORTUNITY FOR MANIFESTING, AND THEREFORE ACQUIRING THE QUALITIES IN WHICH YOUR CHARACTER IS NATURALLY DEFICIENT.

AND THE REFINER SITS PATIENTLY BESIDE THE CRUCIBLE, INTENT ON THE PROCESS, TEMPERING THE HEAT, AND EAGER THAT THE SCUM SHOULD PASS OFF AND HIS OWN FACE BECOME REFLECTED IN THE SURFACE.
— F.B. MEYER

THE TIME WILL COME WHEN, FOR EVERY OUNCE OF PRESENT BURDEN, WE SHALL RECEIVE A FAR MORE EXCEEDING AND ETERNAL WEIGHT OF GLORY!
C.H.S

O BLESS OUR GOD, YE PEOPLE, AND MAKE THE VOICE OF HIS PRAISE BE HEARD: WHICH HOLDETH OUR SOUL IN LIFE, AND SUFFERETH NOT OUR FEET TO BE MOVED.
FOR THOU, O GOD, HAST PROVED US; THOU HAST TRIED US AS SILVER IS TRIED. VV 8-10

Psalm 67

God be merciful unto us, and bless us; and cause His face to shine upon us; Selah!

That Thy way may be known upon the earth, Thy saving health among the nations. Let the people praise Thee, O God; let all the people praise Thee. O let the nations be glad and sing for joy; for Thou shalt judge the people righteously, and govern the nations upon earth. Selah! v.v. 1-4

Nations never will be glad till they follow the leadership of the Great Shepherd. They may shift their modes of government from monarchies to republics, and from republics to communes, but they will retain their wretchedness till they bow before the Lord of All. What a sweet word is that "to sing for joy!" Some sing for form, others for show, some as a duty, others as an amusement, but to sing from the heart, because overflowing joy must find a vent, this is to sing indeed.

Whole nations will do this when Jesus reigns over them in the power of His grace. We have heard hundreds and even thousands sing in chorus, but what will it be to hear whole nations lifting up their voices, as the noise of many waters and like great thunders!

— C.H. Spurgeon

"And all the ends of the earth shall fear Him." v. 7

The far off shall fear. The ends of the earth shall end their idolatry, and adore their God. All tribes, without exception, shall feel a sacred awe of the God of Israel. Ignorance shall be removed, insolence subdued, injustice banished, idolatry abhorred, and the Lord's love, light, life, and liberty, shall be over all, the Lord Himself being King of kings and Lord of lords! Amen and Amen.

Hallelujah! The Lord God omnipotent reigneth! Glory!

Praise God from whom all blessings flow
Praise Him above ye heavenly host
Praise Him all creatures
Praise Father Son and
Now and ever shall be
The Son and to the
Holy, Holy, Holy, Lord God Almighty, which was, and is, and is to come.
World without end. Amen. Holy Ghost
Holy Ghost. Here below.
Glory be to the Father and to
As it was in the beginning

81

PSALM 68

Oh, do not carry your burdens for a single moment longer, pass them over to Him who has already taken your eternal interests to his heart. Only be patient, and wait on Him, and do not run to and fro seeking for help from man, or making men your consolers and confidants. Those who do this have their reward. But as for you, anoint your head and wash your face so as not to excite the pity of others. "Cast thy burden on the Lord, and He will sustain thee." But when it has been cast, leave it with Him.

Refuse to yield to anxious suggestions, and forthwith burst out into a song of thankful confidence. Bless Him! Praise Him! Be glad, and rejoice! When the heart is lightened of its load, it will soar."
—F. B. Meyer

THE EARTH TREMBLED, THE HEAVENS ALSO POURED DOWN RAIN AT THE PRESENCE OF GOD, THE GOD OF ISRAEL... BLESSED BE THE LORD, WHO BEARS OUR BURDENS AND CARRIES US DAY BY DAY, EVEN THE GOD WHO IS OUR SALVATION!... SELAH.. PAUSE AND CALMLY THINK OF THAT! O GOD, AWE-INSPIRING, PROFOUNDLY IMPRESSIVE, AND TERRIBLE ARE YOU OUT OF YOUR HOLY PLACES; THE GOD OF ISRAEL HIMSELF GIVES STRENGTH AND FULLNESS OF MIGHT TO HIS PEOPLE.... BLESSED BE GOD!

PSALM 68: 7, 8, 19, 35

PSALM 69

THE LORD IS CLOSE TO THOSE WHOSE HEARTS ARE BREAKING; HE RESCUES THOSE WHO ARE HUMBLY SORRY FOR THEIR SINS.   PSALM 34:18

HE HEALS THE BROKENHEARTED AND BINDS UP THEIR WOUNDS (CURING THEIR PAINS AND THEIR SORROWS).

PSALM 147:3

INSULTS AND REPROACH HAVE BROKEN MY HEART... ...FOR THE LORD HEARS THE POOR AND NEEDY AND DESPISES NOT HIS PRISONERS (HIS MISERABLE AND WOUNDED ONES)

V.V. 20, 33

HE WAS WOUNDED FOR OUR TRANSGRESSIONS, HE WAS BRUISED FOR OUR GUILT AND INIQUITIES; THE CHASTISEMENT NEEDFUL TO OBTAIN PEACE AND WELL-BEING FOR US WAS UPON HIM, AND WITH HIS STRIPES, THAT WOUNDED HIM, WE ARE HEALED AND MADE WHOLE!

ISAIAH 53:5

PSALM 70

MAKE HASTE O GOD, TO DELIVER ME; MAKE HASTE TO HELP ME, O LORD . . . . LET ALL THOSE WHO SEEK THEE
REJOICE AND BE GLAD IN THEE; AND LET SUCH AS LOVE THY SALVATION SAY CONTINUALLY, LET GOD BE MAGNIFIED! VV. 1, 4
AS AN EAGLE STIRRETH UP HER NEST, FLUTTERETH OVER HER YOUNG, SPREADETH ABROAD HER WINGS, TAKETH
THEM, BEARETH THEM ON HER WINGS . . . .   DEUT. 32:11

THE EAGLE MANIFESTS HER LOVE FOR HER YOUNG, NOT BY DEFENDING THE NEST, BUT BY DESTROYING
IT! THE NEST COULD BECOME TOO COMFORTABLE, AND IF THE LITTLE EAGLES WERE COMPLACENT IN THE
NEST THEY WOULD NEVER LEARN TO FLY. THE WISE OLD MOTHER BIRD TEARS OUT THE SOFT LINING OF THE
NEST SO THAT THE TENDER SKIN OF HER YOUNG IS EXPOSED TO THE ROUGH, HARD TWIGS BENEATH. THE
FLEDGLINGS PROTEST THE PROCESS, BUT IT IS DICTATED BY WISDOM AND UNERRING INSTINCT . . . SO GOD!
HE ALLOWS THE IRRITANTS AND ILLS TO COME . . . ONLY THUS CAN WE LEARN TO SOAR!
                                                                    — JOHN PHILLIPS
INCITED BY THE MOTHER'S ENDEAVOURS, THE EAGLET MAY VENTURE ON THE UNTRIED AIR,
AND LO! THE UNACCUSTOMED WINGS FAIL BENEATH ITS WEIGHT, IT FALLS . . . BUT NOT FAR,
FOR THE MOTHER SWOOPS BENEATH, AND BEARS IT AWAY.
TREMBLING SOUL, GOD IS BENEATH YOU. IF YOUR FAITH FAILS, AND YOU
ARE FALLING, LIKE PETER, INTO A BOTTOMLESS PIT . . . HE WILL CATCH YOU
AND BEAR YOU UP, AND TEACH YOU THE MYSTERY OF THE MORE
ABUNDANT LIFE!
                                                — F. B. MEYER

Psalm 71

Here we see a weak man, but he is in a strong habitation; his security rests upon the tower in which he hides, and is not placed in jeopardy through his personal feebleness.

Fast shut is this castle against all adversaries, its gates they cannot burst open; the drawbridge is up, the portcullis is down, the bars are fast in their places; but, there is a secret door, by which friends of the great Lord can enter at all hours of the day or night, as often as ever they please. There is never an hour when it is unlawful to pray. Mercy's gates stand wide open, and shall do so, till, at the last, the Master of the house has risen up to shut the door.

Believers find their God to be their habitation, strong and accessible, and this is to them a sufficient remedy for all the ills of their mortal life!"

—C. H. Spurgeon

JOY

IN THEE, O LORD, DO I PUT MY TRUST; LET ME NEVER BE PUT TO CONFUSION. DELIVER ME IN THY RIGHTEOUSNESS, AND CAUSE ME TO ESCAPE: INCLINE THINE EAR UNTO ME, AND SAVE ME. BE THOU MY STRONG HABITATION, WHEREUNTO I MAY CONTINUALLY RESORT: THOU HAST GIVEN COMMANDMENT TO SAVE ME, FOR THOU ART MY ROCK AND MY FORTRESS. VV 1-3

LET MY MOUTH BE FILLED WITH THY PRAISE AND WITH THY HONOUR ALL THE DAY. V 8

JESUS

BLESSED BE THE LORD GOD, THE GOD OF ISRAEL, WHO ONLY DOETH WONDROUS THINGS. AND BLESSED BE HIS GLORIOUS NAME FOREVER: AND LET THE WHOLE EARTH BE FILLED WITH HIS GLORY; AMEN AND AMEN. VV 18,19

PSALM 72

Book Three

Psalm 73-89

Psalm 73

BUT IT IS GOOD FOR ME TO DRAW NEAR TO GOD: I HAVE PUT MY TRUST IN THE LORD GOD, THAT I MAY DECLARE ALL THY WORKS. V.28

HAD HE DONE SO AT FIRST HE WOULD NOT HAVE BEEN IMMERSED IN SUCH AFFLICTION; WHEN HE DID SO—HE ESCAPED FROM HIS DILEMMA, AND IF HE CONTINUED TO DO SO HE WOULD NOT FALL INTO THE SAME EVIL AGAIN. THE GREATER OUR NEARNESS TO GOD, THE LESS WE ARE AFFECTED BY THE ATTRACTIONS AND DISTRACTIONS OF EARTH. ACCESS INTO THE MOST HOLY PLACE IS A GREAT PRIVILEGE AND A CURE FOR A MULTITUDE OF ILLS.
—C.H. SPURGEON

TRULY GOD IS GOOD TO ISRAEL EVEN TO SUCH AS ARE OF A CLEAN HEART. BUT AS FOR ME MY FEET WERE ALMOST GONE: MY STEP HAD WELL NIGH SLIPPED.—FOR I WAS ENVIOUS OF THE FOOLISH, WHEN I SAW THE PROSPERITY OF THE WICKED.... UNTIL I WENT INTO THE SANCTUARY OF GOD.—THEN I UNDERSTOOD THEIR END.—SURELY THOU DIDST SET THEM IN SLIPPERY PLACES.—THOU CASTEDST THEM DOWN INTO DISTRUCTION. V 17,18

PSALM 74

REMEMBER!

HERE IS AN ATTITUDE IN PRAYER, WHICH CAN ONLY BE TAKEN WHEN THE SOUL HAS BECOME INTIMATE WITH GOD, AND COME TO CLOSE GRIP WITH HIM. WHEN EVERY OTHER REASON HAS BEEN MARSHALLED, AND EVERY ARGUMENT ALLEGED; WHEN STILL THE ANSWER TARRIES, AND THE CASE IS DESPERATE, THEN TURN TO GOD, AND SAY, "THOU CANST NOT RUN BACK FROM THE TERMS OF THE COVENANT TO WHICH THOU HAST PLEDGED THYSELF.... I CLAIM THAT THOU SHOULDST DO AS THOU HAST SAID."

—F.B. MEYER

REMEMBER THIS, THAT THE ENEMY HATH REPROACHED, O LORD, AND THAT THE FOOLISH PEOPLE HAVE BLASPHEMED THY NAME O DELIVER NOT THE SOUL OF THY TURTLEDOVE UNTO THE MULTITUDE OF THE WICKED; FORGET NOT THE CONGREGATION OF THY POOR FOREVER. HAVE RESPECT UNTO THE COVENANT; FOR THE DARK PLACES OF THE EARTH ARE FULL OF THE HABITATIONS OF CRUELTY. ARISE, O GOD, PLEAD THINE OWN CAUSE; REMEMBER HOW THE FOOLISH MAN REPROACHETH THEE DAILY. VV 18-20, 22

PSALM 75

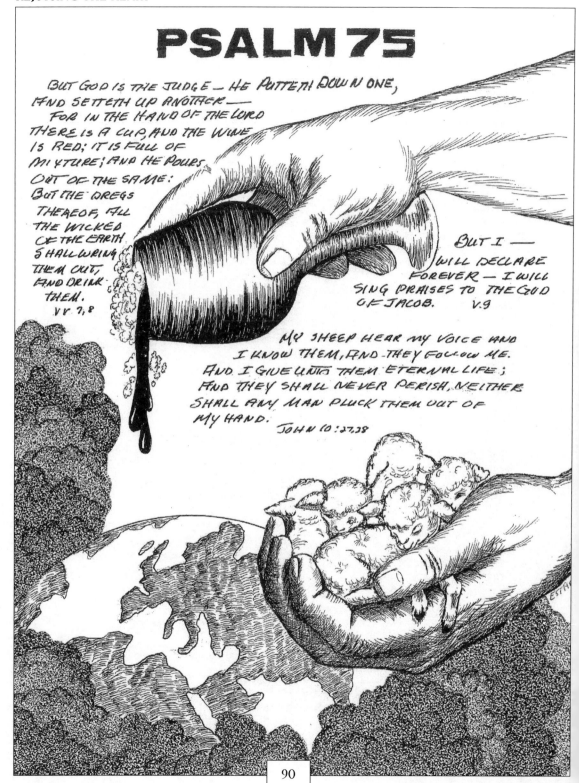

BUT GOD IS THE JUDGE — HE PUTTETH DOWN ONE, AND SETTETH UP ANOTHER —
FOR IN THE HAND OF THE LORD THERE IS A CUP, AND THE WINE IS RED; IT IS FULL OF MIXTURE; AND HE POURS OUT OF THE SAME: BUT THE DREGS THEREOF, ALL THE WICKED OF THE EARTH SHALL WRING THEM OUT, AND DRINK THEM. VV. 7, 8

BUT I — WILL DECLARE FOREVER — I WILL SING PRAISES TO THE GOD OF JACOB. V.9

MY SHEEP HEAR MY VOICE AND I KNOW THEM, AND THEY FOLLOW ME. AND I GIVE UNTO THEM ETERNAL LIFE; AND THEY SHALL NEVER PERISH, NEITHER SHALL ANY MAN PLUCK THEM OUT OF MY HAND. JOHN 10:27,28

PSALM 76

IN JUDAH GOD IS KNOWN AND RENOWNED; HIS
NAME IS HIGHLY PRAISED AND IS GREAT IN ISRAEL.
   IN JERUSALEM ALSO IS HIS TABERNACLE, AND
HIS DWELLING PLACE IS IN ZION. THERE HE BROKE
THE BOWS FLASHING ARROWS, THE SHIELD, THE SWORD
AND THE WEAPONS OF WAR...SELAH!
   HE WILL CUT OFF THE SPIRIT OF PRIDE
AND FURY OF PRINCES; HE IS TERRIBLE TO THE
UNGODLY KINGS OF THE EARTH !   V.V. 1-3, 12

   JEHOVAH IS KNOWN AS THE LION OF THE
TRIBE OF JUDAH. HE IS POWERFUL IN PATIENCE,
..BUT.. FINALLY AROUSED FROM HIS DWELLING
PLACE BY THE SCRATCHING OF THE SHARP LITTLE
CLAWS OF THE RATS OF THIS WORLD, AND
HAVING ENOUGH OF THEIR PATHETIC TAUNTS
AND THREATS ...HE WILL ROAR!
   AT THE FIRST SOUND OF HIS VOICE, THE
VERMIN WILL TURN SCREAMING IN PANIC,
FOR THE LION'S TEETH ARE TERRIBLE!
   OUR KING JESUS IS POWERFUL IN HIS
PATIENCE, BUT THE AGE OF GRACE WILL SOON
COME TO AN END. THE WICKED ONE AND HIS
WHOLE PACK, NOW SO BOLD AND BLASPHEMOUS
IN MURDER AND ABUSE, WILL SCREAM IN
PANIC WHEN KING JESUS COMES FORTH FROM
HIS DWELLING PLACE IN THE CHURCH TO WIPE
THEM OUT AND JUDGE THEIR ABOMINABLE SIN.
   AH, YES!... EVEN THE WRATH OF MAN WILL
ONE DAY PRAISE THE LORD! ALL THE PAIN AND
SUFFERING, MEANT TO DESTROY HIS CHILDREN
IN THE FURNACE OF AFFLICTION WILL
PRODUCE SOMETHING BEAUTIFUL.
   IN THE FLAMING HEAT
ALL THE IMPURITIES WILL
MELT AWAY AND PURE GOLD
WILL RISE TO THE SURFACE. THIS
WILL BE FASHIONED INTO CROWNS;
THOUSANDS OF CROWNS, AND IN
JOYOUS GRATITUDE WE SHALL
LAY THEM AT THE SAVIOUR'S
FEET.

PSALM 77

I cried unto God with my voice, even unto God
with my voice; and he gave ear unto me.
I remembered God, and was troubled:
I complained, and my spirit was overwhelmed. Selah
I will remember the works of the Lord:
surely I will remember thy wonders of old.
The waters saw thee, O God, the waters saw thee;
they were afraid: the depths also were troubled. vv 1, 3, 11, 16

PSALM 78

Yea, they spake against God; they said, Can God furnish a table in the wilderness?
v.19

OH, FATAL QUESTION! IT SHUT ISRAEL OUT OF THE LAND OF PROMISE, AND IT WILL DO AS MUCH FOR YOU. ISRAEL HAD SEEN THE WONDERFUL WORKS OF GOD, CLEAVING THE SEA, LIGHTING THE NIGHT, AND GIVING WATER FROM ROCKS. YET THEY QUESTIONED GODS ABILITY TO GIVE BREAD AND TO SPREAD A TABLE IN THE WILDERNESS. SURELY IT IS A SLUR ON HIS GRACIOUS PROVIDENCE TO SUPPOSE THAT HE HAS BEGUN WHAT HE CANNOT COMPLETE, AND HAS DONE SO MUCH BUT CAN NOT DO ALL!

BUT WE ARE IN DANGER OF MAKING THE SAME MISTAKE. THOUGH BEHIND US LAY THE GIFT OF THE CROSS, THE MIRACLES OF RESURRECTION AND ASCENSION, THE CARE EXERCISED BY GOD OVER OUR EARLY YEARS, WE ARE DISPOSED TO SAY "CAN GOD?"

CAN GOD KEEP ME FROM YIELDING TO THAT BESETTING SIN? CAN GOD FIND ME A SITUATION AND PROVIDE FOOD FOR MY CHILDREN?

CAN GOD EXTRICATE ME FROM THIS TERRIBLE SNARE IN WHICH I AM ENTANGLED?

CAN GOD?

WE LOOK AT THE DIFFICULTIES, THE MANY WHO HAVE SUCCUMBED, THE SURGES THAT ARE ROLLING HIGH, THE POOR DEVIL POSSESSED CHILD, AND WE SAY, "IF YOU CAN DO ANYTHING—HELP US!"

NO, NO! THERE IS NO "IF" WITH GOD; THERE IS NO LIMIT TO HIS ALMIGHTINESS BUT THY UNBELIEF. ...NEVER AGAIN SAY, CAN GOD? BUT GOD CAN!

THOU HAST MADE AND REDEEMED ME, AND THOU CANST NOT FORSAKE THE WORK OF THINE OWN HANDS. ARGUE FROM ALL THE PAST TO THE PRESENT AND FUTURE.

"HIS LOVE IN TIME PAST FORBIDS ME TO THINK
HE WILL LEAVE ME AT LAST IN TROUBLE TO SINK!"
— F.B. MEYER

How oft did they provoke him in the wilderness, and grieve him in the desert! Yea, they turned back and tempted God— and limited the Holy One of Israel vv 40,41

HELP US, O GOD OF OUR SALVATION, FOR THE GLORY OF YOUR NAME!
DELIVER US, FORGIVE US, AND PURGE AWAY OUR SINS FOR YOUR
NAMES SAKE.   V.9

THEN WE YOUR PEOPLE, THE SHEEP OF YOUR
PASTURE, WILL THANK YOU FOREVER AND EVER...
PRAISING YOUR GREATNESS FROM GENERATION TO
GENERATION.   V.13

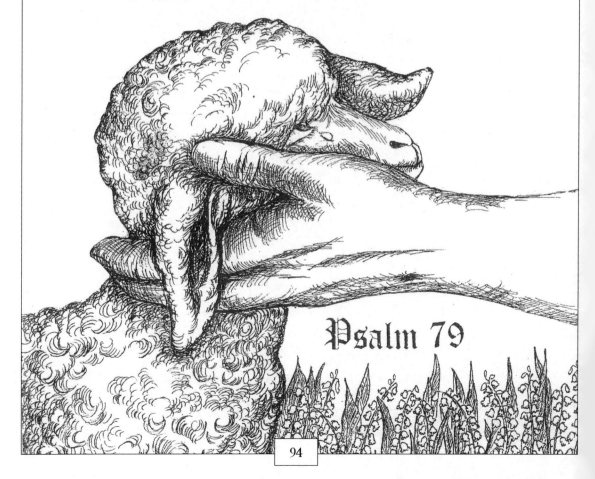

Psalm 79

PSALM 80

THE BRANCH

RETURN, WE BESEECH THEE, O GOD OF HOSTS: LOOK DOWN FROM HEAVEN, AND BEHOLD, AND VISIT THIS VINE; AND THE VINEYARD WHICH THY RIGHT HAND HATH PLANTED, AND THE BRANCH THAT THOU MADEST STRONG FOR THYSELF.

TURN US AGAIN, O LORD GOD OF HOSTS, CAUSE THY FACE TO SHINE; — AND WE SHALL BE SAVED.

V.V 14, 15, 19

AND THERE SHALL COME FORTH A ROD OUT OF THE STEM OF JESSE, AND A BRANCH SHALL GROW OUT OF ITS ROOTS: AND THE SPIRIT OF THE LORD SHALL REST UPON HIM; THE SPIRIT OF WISDOM AND UNDERSTANDING THE SPIRIT OF COUNSEL AND MIGHT, THE SPIRIT OF KNOWLEDGE AND OF THE FEAR OF THE LORD.

ISAIAH 11:1,2

PSALM 81

Sing aloud to God our strength! Shout for joy to the God of Jacob! I am the Lord your God, who brought you up out of the land of Egypt. Open your mouth wide and I will fill it.

God would feed Israel now also with the finest of the wheat; and with honey out of the rock would I satisfy you.   v.v. 1, 10, 16

Because He had brought them out of Egypt He could do great things for them. He had proved His power and His good will; it remained only for His people to believe in Him and ask large things of Him. If their expectations were enlarged to the utmost degree, they could not exceed the bounty of the Lord.... Little birds in the nest open their mouths widely enough, and perhaps the parent birds fail to fill them — but it is never so with our God — His treasures of grace are inexhaustible.   —C. H. Spurgeon

You may easily over-expect the creature, but you cannot over-expect God: "Open thy mouth wide and I will fill it!" Widen and dilate the desires and expectations of your soul and God is able to fill every chink to the vastest capacity. This honours God, when we greaten our expectation of Him.
                              —Thomas Case (1682)

Open thy mouth wide, O Christian, stretch out thy desires to the uttermost, grasp heaven in thy boundless wishes, and believe there is enough in God to afford thee full satisfaction. Not only come, but come with boldness to the throne of grace; it is erected for sinners... those who expect most from God are likely to receive most!
      —Benjamin Beddome

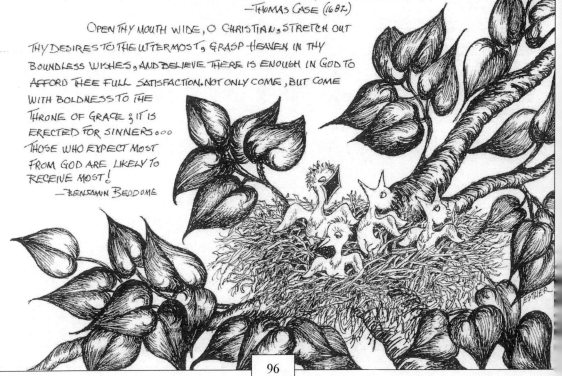

FINALLY!

PSALM 82

THERE IS COMING A DAY..... ITS
 WHEN THE SCALE IN THE HAND
WILL CAREFULLY WEIGH EACH
 LONG BURIED IN YESTERDAYS

COMING FAST,
OF GOD,
ACT OF THE PAST,
SOD.

NOT ONE LUMP FORGOTTEN,
 UNCOVERED, DISPLAYED,
DARK SCHEMES AND RELATION-
 NEITHER SHAME NOR EXCUSE

IGNORED, DISGUISED,
OPENED WIDE!
SHIPS ONCE SO PRIZED,
 WILL HIDE.

ONE GLORIOUS MOMENT THE
 SAINTS WILL GATHER TO
FROM EVERY DIRECTION HIS OWN
 OVERWHELMED WITH JOY

TRUMPET SHALL SOUND,
MEET THE KING,
ARE FOUND,
 THEY WILL SING . . .

"THE GLORIOUS JUDGE HAS
 FINALLY COME!
REJOICE!
 SHOUT FOR JOY!
 DRY YOUR TEAR!
ALL WRONGS ARE MADE RIGHT...
 THE VICTORY'S WON!
HALLELUJAH!
 JESUS IS HERE!"

TRUTH
RIGHTEOUSNESS

SIN
CORRUPTION

ARISE, OH GOD, JUDGE THE EARTH,
FOR THOU SHALT INHERIT ALL NATIONS. V. 8

PSALM 83

KEEP NOT THOU SILENCE, O GOD; HOLD NOT THY PEACE, AND BE NOT STILL, O GOD. FOR, LO, THINE ENEMIES MAKE A TUMULT, AND THEY THAT HATE THEE HAVE LIFTED UP THE HEAD. THEY HAVE TAKEN CRAFTY COUNSEL AGAINST THY PEOPLE, AND CONSULTED AGAINST THY HIDDEN ONES.... O MY GOD, MAKE THEM LIKE A WHEEL, LIKE THE STUBBLE BEFORE THE WIND. AS THE FIRE BURNETH THE FOREST AND AS THE FLAME SETTETH THE MOUNTAINS ON FIRE, SO PERSECUTE THEM WITH THY TEMPEST, AND MAKE THEM AFRAID WITH THY STORM. . . . . THAT MEN MAY KNOW THAT THOU, WHOSE NAME ALONE IS THE LORD, ART THE MOST HIGH OVER ALL THE EARTH!
                                                          VV. 1-3, 13-15, 18

LIKE A RIVER GLORIOUS IS GOD'S PERFECT PEACE, OVER ALL VICTORIOUS IN ITS BRIGHT INCREASE; PERFECT, YET IT FLOWETH FULLER EVERY DAY, PERFECT, YET IT GROWETH DEEPER, ALL THE WAY.

HIDDEN IN THE HOLLOW OF HIS BLESSED HAND, NEVER FOE CAN FOLLOW, NEVER TRAITOR STAND; NOT A SURGE OF WORRY, NOT A SHADE OF CARE, NOT A BLAST OF HURRY TOUCH THE SPIRIT THERE.

EVERY JOY OR TRIAL FALLETH FROM ABOVE, TRACED UPON OUR DIAL BY THE SUN OF LOVE; WE MAY TRUST HIM FULLY ALL FOR US TO DO; THEY WHO TRUST HIM WHOLLY FIND HIM WHOLLY TRUE!

STAYED UPON JEHOVAH, HEARTS ARE FULLY BLESSED; FINDING AS HE PROMISED — PERFECT PEACE AND REST!

PSALM 84

One of the old Puritan writers has well observed that the desires of the heart are the best proofs of our salvation. ...For we cannot counterfeit our longing. We can counterfeit the things we say; ... We can counterfeit the things we do; a good action can be done out of a sense of discipline or duty without our hearts being in it at all. But we cannot counterfeit the things we want.

John, in closing the Revelation, tells of the celestial city: there will be no tears there, no night, no sorrow, no sea, no temple, no sinners. He keeps the best till last, however, and tells us that Jesus will be there: "And they shall see His face!"

That's it! Jesus is there! ...

Our longings are centered in the sanctuary because that is where Jesus is. — JOHN PHILLIPS

How amiable are thy tabernacles O Lord of hosts! My soul longeth, yea, even fainteth for the courts of the Lord; my heart and my flesh cry out for the living God.

Yea, the sparrow hath found an house, and the swallow a nest for herself, where she may lay her young, even thine altars, O Lord of hosts, my King and my God.

Blessed are they who dwell in thy house; they will be still praising thee. 1-4 Selah.

O Lord of hosts, blessed is the man who trusteth in thee. v12

PSALM 85

LORD, THOU HAST BEEN FAVOURABLE UNTO THY LAND; THOU HAST BROUGHT BACK THE CAPTIVITY OF JACOB.
THOU HAST FORGIVEN THE INIQUITY OF THY PEOPLE; THOU HAST COVERED ALL THEIR SIN.
SHEW US THY MERCY, O LORD, AND GRANT US THY SALVATION.
SURELY HIS SALVATION IS NIGH THEM THAT FEAR HIM; THAT GLORY MAY DWELL IN OUR LAND. VV. 1, 2, 7, 9

PSALM 86

FOR THOU, LORD, ART GOOD AND READY TO FORGIVE, AND PLENTEOUS IN MERCY UNTO ALL THOSE WHO CALL UPON THEE V.5

FOR THOU ART GREAT, AND DOEST WONDROUS THINGS — THOU ART GOD ALONE. V.10

FOR GREAT IS THY MERCY TOWARD ME; THOU HAST DELIVERED MY SOUL FROM THE LOWEST HELL. V.13

BUT THOU, O LORD, ART A GOD FULL OF COMPASSION, AND GRACIOUS, LONGSUFFERING, AND PLENTEOUS IN MERCY AND TRUTH. V.15

Fill my cup Lord,
I lift it up, Lord
Come and quench
this thirsting of
my soul . . . . .

NOW UNTO HIM WHO IS ABLE TO DO EXCEEDINGLY ABUNDANTLY ABOVE ALL WE ASK OR THINK, ACCORDING TO THE POWER THAT WORKETH IN US, — UNTO HIM — BE GLORY IN THE CHURCH BY CHRIST JESUS THROUGHOUT ALL AGES, WORLD WITHOUT END. AMEN!

EPH. 3:20, 21

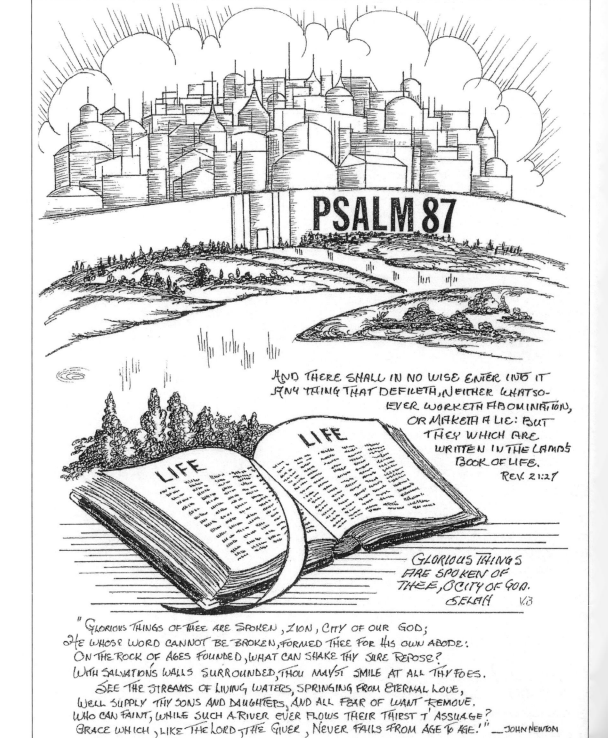

PSALM 87

AND THERE SHALL IN NO WISE ENTER INTO IT ANY THING THAT DEFILETH, NEITHER WHATSOEVER WORKETH ABOMINATION, OR MAKETH A LIE: BUT THEY WHICH ARE WRITTEN IN THE LAMBS BOOK OF LIFE.
REV. 21:27

LIFE

LIFE

GLORIOUS THINGS ARE SPOKEN OF THEE, O CITY OF GOD. SELAH   V.3

" GLORIOUS THINGS OF THEE ARE SPOKEN, ZION, CITY OF OUR GOD;
HE WHOSE WORD CANNOT BE BROKEN, FORMED THEE FOR HIS OWN ABODE:
ON THE ROCK OF AGES FOUNDED, WHAT CAN SHAKE THY SURE REPOSE?
WITH SALVATION'S WALLS SURROUNDED, THOU MAYST SMILE AT ALL THY FOES.
SEE THE STREAMS OF LIVING WATERS, SPRINGING FROM ETERNAL LOVE,
WELL SUPPLY THY SONS AND DAUGHTERS, AND ALL FEAR OF WANT REMOVE.
WHO CAN FAINT, WHILE SUCH A RIVER EVER FLOWS THEIR THIRST T' ASSUAGE?
GRACE WHICH, LIKE THE LORD, THE GIVER, NEVER FAILS FROM AGE TO AGE!"   —JOHN NEWTON

PSALM 88

O GOD OF MY SALVATION
I HAVE CRIED DAY AND NIGH
BEFORE THEE: LET MY PRAYER
COME BEFORE THEE: INCLINE THINE
EAR UNTO MY CRY;
FOR MY SOUL IS FULL OF
TROUBLES: AND MY LIFE DRAWETH
NIGH UNTO THE GRAVE.
THOU HAST LAID ME IN THE
LOWEST PIT, IN DARKNESS, IN
THE DEEPS. THY WRATH LIETH
HARD UPON ME. THOU HAST
AFFLICTED ME WITH ALL THY
WAVES. SELAH   VV 1-3, 6,7

JESUS SAVIOUR PILOT ME
OVER LIFE'S TEMPESTUOUS SEA;
UNKNOWN WAVES BEFORE ME
ROLL, HIDING ROCK AND TREACHEROUS
SHOAL;
CHART AND COMPASS CAME FROM THEE;
JESUS SAVIOUR, PILOT ME.
AS A MOTHER STILLS HER CHILD, THOU CANST HUSH THE OCEAN WILD BOISTEROUS WAVES OBEY
THY WILL WHEN THOU SAYST TO THEM, "BE STILL"; WONDROUS SOVEREIGN OF THE SEA;
JESUS SAVIOUR, PILOT ME.
WHEN AT LAST I NEAR THE SHORE, AND THE FEARFUL BREAKERS ROAR, 'TWIXT ME AND
THE PEACEFUL REST, THEN WHILE LEANING ON THY BREAST, MAY I HEAR THEE SAY TO ME
"FEAR NOT — I WILL PILOT THEE".
—EDWARD HOPPER

PSALM 89

I WILL SING OF THE MERCIES OF THE LORD FOREVER;
WITH MY MOUTH WILL I MAKE KNOWN THY FAITHFULNESS TO ALL GENERATIONS.
FOR I HAVE SAID, MERCY SHALL BE BUILT UP FOREVER;
THY FAITHFULNESS SHALT THOU ESTABLISH IN THE VERY HEAVENS.
  I HAVE MADE A COVENANT WITH MY CHOSEN, I HAVE SWORN UNTO DAVID,
MY SERVANT;
  THY SEED WILL I ESTABLISH FOREVER, AND BUILD UP THY THRONE TO ALL
GENERATIONS. SELAH   VS 1-4
-- ALSO I WILL MAKE HIM MY FIRST BORN, HIGHER THAN THE KINGS OF THE EARTH.
HIS SEED ALSO WILL I MAKE TO ENDURE FOREVER, AND HIS THRONE AS THE
DAYS OF HEAVEN   VS. 27 & 29

FOR UNTO US A CHILD IS BORN,
UNTO US A SON IS GIVEN; AND
THE GOVERNMENT SHALL
BE UPON HIS SHOULDER;
AND HIS NAME SHALL
BE CALLED . . . . . .
WONDERFUL,
COUNSELOR,
THE MIGHTY GOD,
THE EVERLASTING
FATHER,
THE PRINCE OF PEACE.
ISAIAH 9:6

Book Four

Psalm 90-106

PSALM 90

Lord, Thou hast been our dwelling place in all generations. Before the mountains were brought forth, or ever Thou hadst formed the earth and the world, even from everlasting to everlasting — Thou art God. — 1,2

So teach us to number our days that we may apply our hearts unto wisdom. — 12

O God, our help in ages past, our hope for years to come,
Our shelter from the stormy blast, and our eternal home!
Under the shadow of Thy throne Thy saints have dwelt secure;
Sufficient is Thine arm alone, and our defense is sure.
Before the hills in order stood, or earth received her frame,
From everlasting Thou art God, to endless years the same.
A thousand ages in Thy sight are like an evening gone;
Short as the watch that ends the night before the rising sun.
O God, our help in ages past —— Our hope for years to come,
Be Thou our guard while life shall last —— And our eternal home.
— ISAAC WATTS

SAFE Psalm 91

HE THAT DWELLETH IN THE SECRET PLACE OF THE MOST HIGH SHALL ABIDE UNDER THE SHADOW OF THE ALMIGHTY. I WILL SAY OF THE LORD, HE IS MY REFUGE AND MY FORTRESS: MY GOD; IN HIM WILL I TRUST.

VV 1,2

HE SHALL COVER THEE WITH HIS FEATHERS; AND UNDER HIS WINGS SHALT THOU TRUST: HIS TRUTH SHALL BE THY SHIELD AND BUCKLER. THOU SHALT NOT BE AFRAID FOR THE TERROR BY NIGHT; NOR FOR THE ARROW THAT FLIETH BY DAY;

VV 4,5

PSALM 92

IT IS A GOOD THING TO GIVE
THANKS UNTO THE LORD, TO
SING PRAISES UNTO THY NAME,
O MOST HIGH:
TO SHEW FORTH THY
LOVING KINDNESS IN THE
MORNING, AND THY FAITH-
-FULNESS EVERY NIGHT.
FOR THOU LORD HAST
MADE ME GLAD THROUGH
THY WORK: I WILL TRIUMPH
IN THE WORKS OF THY
HANDS.
O LORD, HOW GREAT
ARE THY WORKS! AND
THY THOUGHTS ARE VERY
DEEP.
VV 1, 2, 4, 5

THE RIGHTEOUS SHALL FLOURISH LIKE THE
PALM TREE: HE SHALL GROW LIKE A CEDAR
IN LEBANON. THOSE THAT BE PLANTED
IN THE HOUSE OF THE LORD SHALL
FLOURISH IN THE COURTS OF OUR GOD.
THEY SHALL STILL BRING FORTH FRUIT IN
OLD AGE: THEY SHALL BE FAT AND FLOURISHING
TO SHEW THAT THE LORD IS UPRIGHT:
HE IS MY ROCK, AND THERE IS NO UNRIGHTEOUSNESS
IN HIM.   VV 12-15

FOR WHICH CAUSE
WE FAINT NOT;
BUT THOUGH OUR
OUTWARD MAN
PERISH, YET...
THE INWARD MAN
IS RENEWED DAY
BY DAY. 2 COR 4:16
THIS IS AN
INTERNAL SPIRITUAL
STRENGTH THAT
ONLY THOSE WHO
HAVE GROWN OLD
WALKING WITH
JESUS AND
TRUSTING JESUS
KNOW. IT GOES
BEYOND HUMAN
UNDERSTANDING
—J.M BOICE

BOOK THREE

JEHOVAH is KING !

THE LORD REIGNETH!
HE IS CLOTHED WITH
MAJESTY:
THE LORD IS CLOTHED
WITH STRENGTH,
WHEREWITH HE HATH
GIRDED HIMSELF:
THE WORLD ALSO IS
ESTABLISHED,
THAT IT CANNOT BE
MOVED.   V.1

THE LORD ON HIGH
IS MIGHTIER THAN THE
NOISE OF MANY WATERS,
YEA, THAN THE MIGHTY
WAVES OF THE SEA.
THY TESTIMONIES
ARE VERY SURE:
HOLINESS BECOMETH
THINE HOUSE,
O LORD,
FOREVER.
W 4-5

WHATEVER TURMOIL AND
REBELLION THERE MAY BE BENEATH
THE CLOUDS, THE ETERNAL KING SITS ABOVE
ALL IN SUPREME SERENITY; AND EVERYWHERE
HE IS REALLY MASTER, LET HIS FOES RAGE AS THEY
MAY———
OUR GOD REIGNS!
—C.H.S.

PSALM 93

PSALM 94
JESUS REIGNS!

IN THE MIDST OF ALL THE TURMOIL,
IN THE MIDDLE OF THE STORM,
IN THE TERROR OF THE DARKNESS,
THIS ONE THOUGHT STANDS STRONG AND FIRM
OUR GOD REIGNS! HALLELUJAH!
OUR GOD REIGNS!

ABOVE THE ROLLING CLOUDS OF WAR,
ABOVE THE ATHEIST'S SCREAMING VOICE,
ABOVE WINDS AND WAVES OF TROUBLE,
STEP UP HIGHER AND REJOICE.
OUR GOD REIGNS! HALLELUJAH!
OUR GOD REIGNS!

SING IT SOFTLY TO THE GRIEVING,
SHOUT TO THE DROWNING MAN AT SEA,
WHISPER TO THE BROKEN HEARTED;
"IN THE MORNING YOU WILL SEE —
OUR GOD REIGNS! HALLELUJAH!
OUR GOD REIGNS!
— Esther

O LORD GOD, TO WHOM
VENGEANCE BELONGETH;
O GOD, TO WHOM VENGEANCE
BELONGETH... SHEW THYSELF.
LIFT UP THYSELF: THOU
JUDGE OF THE EARTH:
RENDER A REWARD TO THE
PROUD.   VV 1,2

Psalm 95

O COME, LET US SING UNTO THE LORD; LET US MAKE A JOYFUL NOISE TO THE ROCK OF OUR SALVATION. LET US COME BEFORE HIS PRESENCE WITH THANKSGIVING, AND MAKE A JOYFUL NOISE WITH PSALMS. FOR THE LORD IS A GREAT GOD, AND A GREAT KING ABOVE ALL GODS. IN HIS HAND ARE THE DEEP PLACES OF THE EARTH; THE STRENGTH OF THE HILLS IS HIS ALSO. THE SEA IS HIS, AND HE MADE IT; AND HIS HANDS FORMED THE DRY LAND. VV 1-5

HOW GREAT THOU ART!
GOD'S MIGHT IS EVERYWHERE DISPLAYED.
THE PSALMIST TELLS US TO PLUMB THE DEPTHS,
TO DIG DEEP. FOR "IN HIS HAND ARE THE DEEP
PLACES OF THE EARTH." HE INVITES US TO CLIMB
THE HEIGHTS, TO SCALE THE LOFTY MOUNTAINS,
TO PLANT OUR FEET ON HIGHER GROUND.
-JOHN PHILLIPS

PSALM 96

SING!

SING UNTO THE LORD A NEW SONG; SING UNTO THE LORD, ALL THE EARTH. SING UNTO THE LORD, BLESS HIS NAME; SHEW FORTH HIS SALVATION FROM DAY TO DAY. DECLARE HIS GLORY AMONG THE HEATHEN; HIS WONDERS AMONG ALL PEOPLE. LET THE HEAVENS REJOICE; AND LET THE EARTH BE GLAD; LET THE SEA ROAR, AND THE FULLNESS THEREOF. LET THE FIELD BE JOYFUL, AND ALL THAT IS THEREIN; THEN SHALL THE TREES OF THE WOOD REJOICE BEFORE THE LORD; FOR HE COMETH TO JUDGE THE EARTH; HE SHALL JUDGE THE WORLD WITH RIGHTEOUSNESS, AND THE PEOPLE WITH TRUTH.

VV 1-3, 11-13

ESTHER

"JESUS, JESUS, JESUS, SWEETEST NAME I KNOW, FILLS MY EVERY LONGING, KEEPS ME SINGING AS I GO!"

PSALM 97

JESUS REIGNS

The Lord reigneth; let the earth rejoice; let the multitude of isles be glad thereof. Clouds and darkness are round about him: righteousness and judgment are the habitation of his throne. A fire goeth before him, and burneth up his enemies round about. His lightnings enlightened the world: the earth saw, and trembled. The hills melted like wax at the presence of the Lord, at the presence of the Lord of the whole earth. Vs. 1-5

"A fire goeth before him." Like an advance guard clearing the way. So was it at Sinai, so must it be: the very Being of God is power, consuming all opposition; omnipotence is a devouring flame which "burneth up his enemies round about." God is longsuffering, but when he comes forth to judgment he will make short work with the unrighteous, they will be as chaff before the flame. Reading this verse in reference to the coming of Jesus, and the descent of the Spirit, we are reminded of the tongues of fire, and of the power which attended the gospel, so that all opposition was speedily overcome. Even now where the gospel is preached in faith, and in the power of the Spirit, it burns its own way, irresistibly destroying falsehood, superstition, unbelief, sin, indifference, and the hardness of heart. In it the Lord reigneth, and because of it let the earth rejoice. John Phillips

A Glimpse of Glory!

PSALM 98

THE COMING OF THE KING

MAKE A JOYFUL SYMPHONY BEFORE THE LORD, THE KING! LET THE SEA AND EVERYTHING IN IT SHOUT HIS PRAISE! LET THE EARTH AND ALL LIVING THINGS JOIN IN........... FOR THE LORD IS COMING TO JUDGE THE EARTH! v.6,7,8

Psalm 99

BUT AS HE WHICH HAS CALLED YOU IS HOLY, SO BE YE HOLY IN ALL MANNER OF CONVERSATION BECAUSE IT IS WRITTEN, BE YE HOLY; FOR I AM HOLY.

HOLY HOLY HOLY

HOLY, HOLY, HOLY, IS THE LORD GOD ALMIGHTY, WHO WAS, AND IS, AND IS TO COME. REV. 4:8

HOLY HOLY HOLY IS THE LORD GOD ALMIGHTY THE WHOLE EARTH IS FULL OF HIS GLORY ISAIAH 6:3

THE LORD REIGNETH

LET THE PEOPLE TREMBLE; HE SITTETH BETWEEN THE CHERUBIMS; LET THE EARTH BE MOVED. THE LORD IS GREAT IN ZION; AND HE IS HIGH ABOVE ALL THE PEOPLE. LET THEM PRAISE THY GREAT AND TERRIBLE NAME; FOR IT IS HOLY. EXALT YE THE LORD OUR GOD AND WORSHIP AT HIS FOOTSTOOL... FOR HE IS HOLY! VV 1-3, 5

PSALM 100

ENTER
INTO HIS GATES WITH
THANKSGIVING,
AND INTO HIS COURTS
WITH PRAISE;
BE THANKFUL UNTO HIM,
AND BLESS HIS NAME,
FOR.....
THE LORD IS GOOD; HIS
MERCY IS EVERLASTING,
AND HIS TRUTH ENDURETH
TO ALL GENERATIONS! VV. 4,5

THERE ARE TIMES WHEN WE FEEL DRY, POWERLESS, AND DOWNHEARTED
— EVEN THOUGH WE PRAY. HOW CAN THIS BE ?
THE FATHER WHISPERS GENTLY, "YOU STAND TOO FAR AWAY, OUTSIDE THE
GATE, COME CLOSE, DEAR ONE, USE THE KEY — IT IS SO BEAUTIFUL INSIDE!"

PSALM 101

The Will

"TO BE PERFECTLY COURTEOUS TO THOSE WHOM YOU ARE MEETING AT EVERY MEAL; TO HOLD YOURSELF UNDER PERFECT CONTROL WHEN WORRIED BY INSIDIOUS JARS AND STUNG BY ALMOST INVISIBLE GNATS; TO MAINTAIN ALWAYS THE PERFECT GIRDING OF THE LOINS; TO HAVE THE HEAD ALWAYS ANOINTED AND THE FACE ALWAYS WASHED, TO REALIZE GOD'S IDEAL...LOVE'S IDEAL...AND YOUR OWN...AH, ME! THIS REQUIRES THE UTMOST GRACE THAT GOD CAN GIVE...TO DIE ONCE IS EASY-TO LIVE ALWAYS WITH AN UNDIVIDED HEART-THIS IS HARD! UNDERSTAND THAT IN THE HOMELIFE GOD IS EDUCATING AND TRAINING YOU FOR THE GREATEST VICTORIES!"

F. B. MEYER

I WILL SING OF MERCY AND JUDGEMENT; UNTO THEE, O LORD, WILL I SING. I WILL BEHAVE MYSELF WISELY IN A PERFECT WAY O WHEN WILT THOU COME UNTO ME? I WILL WALK WITHIN MY HOUSE WITH A PERFECT HEART.

I WILL SET NO WICKED THING BEFORE MINE EYES: I HATE THE WORK OF THEM THAT TURN ASIDE; IT SHALL NOT CLEAVE TO ME. VV1-3

FEELINGS

" THE SMOKE-WREATH DISSIPATED IN THE BREEZE, THE WITHERED GRASS OF THE DESERT, THE DECLINING SHADOW — THE CHIRRUP OF A LONELY SPARROW — SUCH ARE THE IMAGES THAT OCCUR NATURALLY ENOUGH. BUT AS HE SINGS THE MAN'S VISION CLEARS. HE LOOKS AWAY FROM EARTH-MISTS TO THE ETERNAL GOD!

HERE AT LEAST, IS THE PERMANENT AND UNCHANGING. DID HE MAKE ALL THINGS? THEN HE CAN UNMAKE THEM, AND BE HIMSELF EVERMORE THE SAME!

LET THE EARTH VANISH LIKE A DREAM; LET THE TIME-SPHERE BE ENDED; LET THE VERY HEAVENS WEAR OUT LIKE A MOTH-EATEN GARMENT; LET THE NEAREST AND DEAREST PASS FROM OUR EMBRACE... THOU ART THE SAME;
            THOU ART LEFT;
            THOU REMAINEST!"
                    — F.B. MEYER

BUT THOU, O LORD, SHALT ENDURE FOREVER, AND THY REMEMBRANCE UNTO ALL GENERATIONS.   V. 12
BUT THOU ART THE SAME, AND THY YEARS SHALL HAVE NO END!
                                V 27

PSALM 102

BLESS THE LORD,
O MY SOUL; AND ALL THAT IS WITHIN
ME, BLESS HIS HOLY NAME.

BLESS THE LORD, O MY SOUL, AND FORGET NOT
ALL HIS BENEFITS:
  WHO FORGIVETH ALL THY INIQUITIES ....
  WHO HEALETH ALL THY DISEASES ....
  WHO REDEEMETH THY LIFE FROM DESTRUCTION ....
  WHO CROWNETH THEE WITH LOVING-KINDNESS AND TENDER MERCIES ....
  WHO SATISFIETH THY MOUTH WITH GOOD THINGS, SO THAT
THY YOUTH IS RENEWED LIKE THE EAGLE'S.

THUS IS THE ENDLESS CHAIN OF GRACE COMPLETE — SIN IS FORGIVEN,
ITS POWER SUBDUED, AND ITS PENALTY AVERTED, THEN ARE WE
HONORED, SUPPLIED, AND OUR VERY NATURE RENOVATED, TILL WE ARE
AS NEW-BORN CHILDREN IN THE HOUSEHOLD OF GOD!
  O LORD, WE MUST BLESS THEE — AND WE WILL; AS THOU DOST WITH-
HOLD NOTHING FROM US, SO WE WOULD NOT KEEP BACK FROM THY PRAISE
ONE SOLITARY POWER OF OUR NATURE, BUT WITH ALL OUR HEART, AND
SOUL, AND STRENGTH PRAISE THY HOLY NAME!   — C.H. SPURGEON

HE BREAKS THE POWER OF CANCELED SIN,
  BLESSED BE THE NAME OF THE LORD!
HIS BLOOD CAN MAKE THE FOULEST CLEAN,
  BLESSED BE THE NAME OF THE LORD!
BLESSED BE THE NAME, BLESSED BE THE NAME,
BLESSED BE THE NAME OF THE LORD!
                      — CHARLES WESLEY

PSALM 103

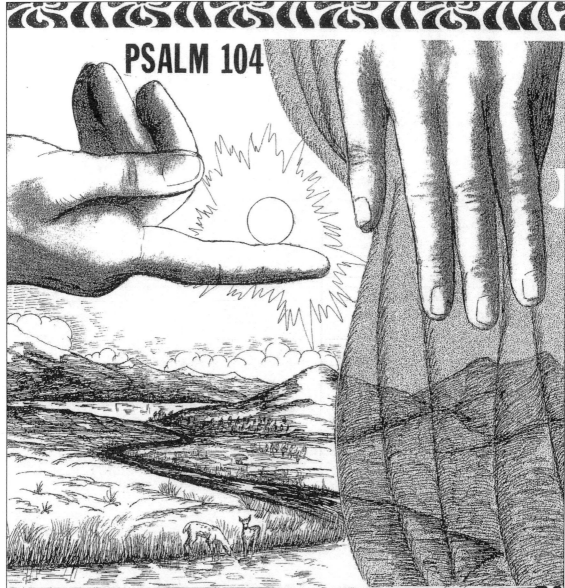

PSALM 104

Bless the Lord, O my soul...O lord my God, Thou art very great; Thou art clothed with honor and magesty.
Who coverest Thyself with light as with a garment; Who stretchest out the heavens like a curtain. (1-2)
He appointed the moon for seasons; the sun knoweth its going down....Thou makest darkness, and it is night, wherein all the beasts of the forest do creep forth. (19-20)

PSALM 105

He spread a cloud for a covering, and fire to give light in the night.

The people asked, and He brought quails, and satisfied them with the bread of heaven.

He opened the rock, and the waters gushed out; they ran in the dry places like a river;

For He remembered His holy promise, and Abraham His servant.

And He brought forth His people with joy, and His chosen with gladness... 39-43

God Himself was their sun and shield — their glory, their defence, and their sufficiency! So He is to us!

PSALM 106

PRAISE YE THE LORD.

O GIVE THANKS UNTO THE LORD; FOR HE IS GOOD: FOR HIS MERCY ENDURETH FOREVER.

WHO CAN UTTER THE MIGHTY ACTS OF THE LORD? WHO CAN SHEW FORTH ALL HIS PRAISE? BLESSED ARE THEY THAT KEEP JUDGE-MENT, AND HE THAT DOETH RIGHTEOUSNESS AT ALL TIMES...

... THEY SOON FORGOT HIS WORKS THEY WAITED NOT FOR HIS COUNSEL; BUT LUSTED EXCEEDINGLY IN THE WILDERNESS, AND TEMPTED GOD IN THE DESERT. AND HE GAVE THEM THEIR REQUEST; BUT SENT LEANNESS INTO THEIR SOUL.

VV 1-3, 13-15

GODS WILL MY WILL

"ISRAEL INSISTED ON BEING FED, NOT WITH MANNA ONLY, BUT WITH FLESH... THEY HAD THEIR DESIRE BUT THEIR SOULS WERE STARVED. OH, DO NOT SEEK TO IMPOSE YOUR WILL ON GOD; DO NOT INSIST ON ANYTHING WITH TOO GREAT VEHEMENCE... LET GOD CHOOSE!"
—F.B. MEYER

122

Book Five

Psalm 107-150

PSALM 107

They reel to and fro, and stagger like a drunken man, and are at their wits' end — all their wisdom has come to nothing.

Then they cry to the Lord in their trouble, and He brings them out of their distresses.

He hushes the storm to a calm and to a gentle whisper, so that the waves of the sea are still.

vs. 27-29

Are you standing at "Wits' End Corner",
 Christian, with troubled brow?
Are you thinking of what is before you,
 And all you are bearing now?
Does all the world seem against you,
 And you in the battle alone?
Remember — at "Wits' End Corner"
 Is just where God's power is shown.

Are you standing at "Wits' End Corner",
 Your work before you spread,
All lying begun, unfinished,
 And pressing on heart and head,
Longing for strength to do it,
 Stretching out trembling hands?
Remember — at "Wits' End Corner"
 The burden-bearer stands.

Are you standing at "Wits' End Corner",
 Then you're just in the very spot
To learn the wondrous resources
 Of Him who faileth not;
No doubt to a brighter pathway
 Your footsteps will soon be moved,
But only at "Wits' End Corner"
 Is "the" God who is able "proved.

— Antoinette Wilson

ESTHER

PSALM 109

HOLD NOT THY PEACE, O GOD OF MY PRAISE:

BUT DO THOU FOR ME, O GOD THE LORD, FOR THY NAME'S SAKE: BECAUSE THY MERCY IS GOOD, DELIVER THOU ME.

FOR I AM POOR AND NEEDY AND MY HEART IS WOUNDED WITHIN ME.

HELP ME, O LORD MY GOD: O SAVE ME ACCORDING TO THY MERCY.

V 1, 21, 22
26

...BUT I GIVE MYSELF UNTO PRAYER
V. 4

I WILL GREATLY PRAISE THE LORD WITH MY MOUTH:
YEA, I WILL PRAISE HIM AMONG THE MULTITUDE.
FOR HE SHALL STAND AT THE RIGHT HAND OF THE POOR, TO SAVE HIM FROM THOSE THAT CONDEMN HIS SOUL.
VV 30, 31

HE IT IS THAT SHALL TREAD DOWN OUR ADVERSARIES!
PSALM 108:13
THIS IS THE WAY TO FIGHT. KEEP QUIETLY IN FELLOWSHIP WITH GOD; AND WHEN THE ENEMY DRAWS NIGH, LOOK UP TO YOUR EVER-PRESENT FRIEND, AND SAY, "NOW, LORD, NOW TREAD DOWN THIS ADVERSARY!"
— F.B. MEYER

THE COMING OF THE
PRIEST - KING - JUDGE!
PSALM 110

THE LORD SAID UNTO MY LORD, SIT THOU AT MY RIGHT HAND,
UNTIL I MAKE THINE ENEMIES THY FOOTSTOOL.
THE LORD SHALL SEND THE ROD OF THY STRENGTH OUT OF ZION.
— RULE THOU IN THE MIDST OF THINE ENEMIES. VV 1,2

IT IS FINISHED!

PSALM III

PRAISE YE THE LORD. I WILL PRAISE
THE LORD WITH MY WHOLE HEART,
IN THE ASSEMBLY OF THE UPRIGHT,
AND IN THE CONGREGATION.
THE WORKS OF THE LORD ARE GREAT,
SOUGHT OUT OF ALL THEM THAT
HAVE PLEASURE THEREIN.
   HIS WORK IS HONORABLE AND
GLORIOUS; AND HIS RIGHTEOUSNESS
ENDURES FOREVER.
HE HATH MADE HIS WONDERFUL
WORKS TO BE REMEMBERED: THE LORD
IS GRACIOUS AND FULL OF COMPASSION.

   HE SENT REDEMPTION UNTO HIS
PEOPLE: HE HATH COMMANDED HIS
COVENANT FOREVER.
HOLY AND REVEREND IS HIS NAME.

VV 1-4, 9

Psalm 112

Praise ye the Lord! Blessed is the man who feareth the Lord, who delighted greatly in His Commandments. His seed shall be mighty upon the earth; the generation of the upright shall be blessed. Vv 1,2
Surely he shall not be moved forever; the righteous shall be in everlasting remembrance. He shall not be afraid of evil tidings....His heart is fixed, trusting in the Lord. His heart is established....He shall not be afraid, until he sees his desire upon his enemies. Vv 6-8

"Tidings! Tidings! They are always pouring in by letter, postcard, and telegram.....but does not the Christian suffer anguish and pain a others do?
Is he stoical and unimpassioned, dull in his emotions, unsympathetic in his affections?
Not so...but he refuses to judge things by appearances. He knows that all things must be working for good on his behalf: in the hieroglyphics
he detects his Father's handwriting.
                            —F.B. Meyer

Therefore whosoever heareth these sayings of mine, and doeth them, I will liken him unto a wise man, which built his house upon a rock: and the rain descended, and the floods came, and the winds blew, and beat upon that house; and it fell not: for it was founded upon a rock. Matthew 7: 24-25

PSALM 113

Praise ye the Lord. Praise, O ye servants of the Lord, praise the name of the Lord. Blessed be the name of the Lord from this time forth and for evermore. From the rising of the sun unto the going down of the same the Lord's name is to be praised. Vv. 1-3

JESUS CHRIST

THE   NAME!

JEHOVAH

Elohim   Adonai

Rapha   Rohi

Shalom   Shammah

Jireh   Nissi

Tsidkenu   M'kadesh

El Shaddai   ABBA Sabaoth

"Throughout the entire Old Testament age God revealed Himself through His names....Name after name, revelation after revelation, until, at last we cross the great divide from the Old Testament to the New and learn the name "Our Father." So when the psalmist tells us to praise the name of the Lord from this time forth and for evermore, it is because His name is the manifold expression of who He is." ~John Philips

PSALM 114

THE MOUNTAINS SKIPPED LIKE RAMS, AND THE LITTLE HILLS LIKE LAMBS. TREMBLE THOU EARTH AT THE PRESENCE OF THE LORD, AT THE PRESENCE OF THE GOD OF JACOB. vv 4,7

"DO WE NOT OURSELVES EXPECT ANOTHER COMING OF THE LORD, WHEN BEFORE HIS FACE HEAVEN AND EARTH SHALL FLEE AWAY AND THERE SHALL BE NO MORE SEA? WE JOIN THEN WITH THE SINGERS AROUND THE PASSOVER TABLE AND MAKE THEIR HALLEL OURS, FOR WE TOO HAVE BEEN LED OUT OF BONDAGE AND GUIDED LIKE A FLOCK THROUGH A DESERT LAND, WHEREIN THE LORD SUPPLIES OUR WANTS WITH HEAVENLY MANNA AND WATER FROM THE ROCK OF AGES... PRAISE YE THE LORD!"

—C. H. SPURGEON

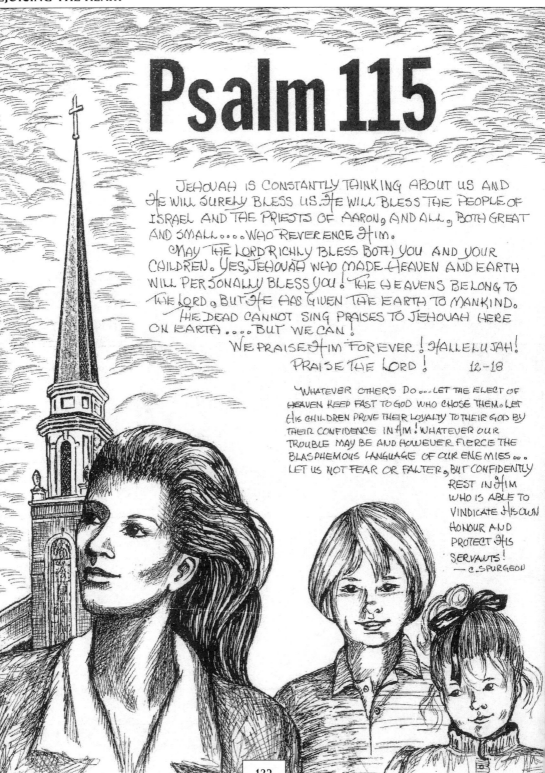

Psalm 115

JEHOVAH IS CONSTANTLY THINKING ABOUT US AND HE WILL SURELY BLESS US. HE WILL BLESS THE PEOPLE OF ISRAEL AND THE PRIESTS OF AARON, AND ALL, BOTH GREAT AND SMALL....WHO REVERENCE HIM.

MAY THE LORD RICHLY BLESS BOTH YOU AND YOUR CHILDREN. YES, JEHOVAH WHO MADE HEAVEN AND EARTH WILL PERSONALLY BLESS YOU! THE HEAVENS BELONG TO THE LORD, BUT HE HAS GIVEN THE EARTH TO MANKIND.

THE DEAD CANNOT SING PRAISES TO JEHOVAH HERE ON EARTH.....BUT WE CAN!

WE PRAISE HIM FOREVER! HALLELUJAH!

PRAISE THE LORD!   12-18

WHATEVER OTHERS DO...LET THE ELECT OF HEAVEN KEEP FAST TO GOD WHO CHOSE THEM. LET HIS CHILDREN PROVE THEIR LOYALTY TO THEIR GOD BY THEIR CONFIDENCE IN HIM! WHATEVER OUR TROUBLE MAY BE AND HOWEVER FIERCE THE BLASPHEMOUS LANGUAGE OF OUR ENEMIES... LET US NOT FEAR OR FALTER, BUT CONFIDENTLY REST IN HIM WHO IS ABLE TO VINDICATE HIS OWN HONOUR AND PROTECT HIS SERVANTS!
— C. SPURGEON

PSALM 116

I LOVE THE LORD, BECAUSE HE HATH HEARD MY VOICE AND MY SUPPLICATIONS. BECAUSE HE HATH INCLINED HIS EAR UNTO ME, THEREFORE WILL I CALL UPON HIM AS LONG AS I LIVE.

THE SORROWS OF DEATH COMPASSED ME, AND THE PAINS OF HELL GAT HOLD OF ME: I FOUND TROUBLE AND SORROW.

THEN CALLED I UPON THE NAME OF THE LORD: O LORD, I BESEECH THEE, DELIVER MY SOUL.

GRACIOUS IS THE LORD, AND RIGHTEOUS...

—YEA, OUR GOD IS MERCIFUL. VV. 1-5

THE LORD PRESERVETH THE SIMPLE...I WAS BROUGHT LOW AND HE HELPED ME. V6

YES, THOSE WHO HAVE A GREAT DEAL OF WIT MAY TAKE CARE OF THEMSELVES. THOSE WHO HAVE NO WORLDLY CRAFT AND SUBTLETY AND GUILE, BUT SIMPLY TRUST IN GOD, AND DO RIGHT MAY DEPEND UPON IT THAT GOD'S CARE WILL BE OVER THEM...... THOUGH THE SAINTS ARE LIKE SHEEP IN THE MIDST OF WOLVES AND COMPARATIVELY DEFENCELESS YET THERE ARE MORE SHEEP IN THE WORLD, AND IT IS HIGHLY PROBABLE THAT THE SHEEP WILL FEED IN SAFETY WHEN NOT A SINGLE WOLF IS LEFT UPON THE FACE OF THE EARTH! EVEN SO THE MEEK SHALL INHERIT THE EARTH, WHEN THE WICKED SHALL BE NO MORE. — C.H. SPURGEON

133

THE UNIVERSAL PRAISE OF GOD

PSALM 117

"WE KNOW AND BELIEVE THAT NO ONE TRIBE OF MEN SHALL BE UNREPRESENTED IN THE UNIVERSAL SONG WHICH SHALL ASCEND UNTO THE LORD OF ALL. INDIVIDUALS HAVE ALREADY BEEN GATHERED OUT OF EVERY KINDRED AND PEOPLE AND TONGUE BY THE PREACHING OF THE GOSPEL, AND THESE HAVE RIGHT HEARTILY JOINED IN MAGNIFYING THE GRACE WHICH SOUGHT THEM OUT, AND BROUGHT THEM TO KNOW THE SAVIOUR. THESE ARE BUT THE ADVANCE-GUARD OF A NUMBER WHICH NO MAN CAN NUMBER WHO WILL COME ERE LONG TO WORSHIP THE ALL-GLORIOUS ONE!"
— C.H. SPURGEON

"COULD WE WITH INK THE OCEAN FILL, AND WERE THE SKIES OF PARCHMENT MADE; WERE EVERY STALK ON EARTH A QUILL, AND EVERY MAN A SCRIBE BY TRADE; TO WRITE THE LOVE OF GOD ABOVE WOULD DRAIN THE OCEAN DRY; NOR COULD THE SCROLL CONTAIN THE WHOLE, THO' STRETCHED FROM SKY TO SKY.
OH, LOVE OF GOD, HOW RICH AND PURE! HOW MEASURELESS AND STRONG! IT SHALL FOREVERMORE ENDURE — THE SAINTS' AND ANGELS' SONG."
— F.M. LEHMAN

PRAISE

PRAISE THE LORD

PRAISE THE LORD

OH, PRAISE THE LORD, YE NATIONS

PRAISE HIM, ALL YE PEOPLE,

FOR HIS MERCIFUL KINDNESS IS GREAT TOWARD US; AND THE TRUTH OF THE LORD ENDURETH FOREVER.....PRAISE YE THE LORD.

PRAISE

GOD IS THE LORD, WHO
HATH SHOWN US LIGHT:
BIND THE SACRIFICE
WITH CORDS, EVEN UNTO
THE HORNS OF THE ALTAR.
v.27

I BESEECH YOU THEREFORE,
BRETHREN, BY THE MERCIES OF
GOD, THAT YE PRESENT YOUR
BODIES A LIVING SACRIFICE,
HOLY, ACCEPTABLE UNTO
GOD.   ROMANS 12:1

For
The Love of Christ
Constraineth us.
2 Cor. 5:14
Psalm 118.

WE BRING OURSELVES TO HIS ALTAR, AND DESIRE TO OFFER HIM
ALL THAT WE HAVE AND ARE. THERE REMAINS A TENDENCY IN OUR
NATURE TO START ASIDE FROM THIS; IT IS NOT FOND OF THE SACRIFICIAL
KNIFE. IN THE WARMTH OF OUR LOVE WE COME WILLINGLY TO THE ALTAR,
BUT WE NEED CONSTRAINING POWER TO KEEP US THERE IN THE ENTIRETY
OF OUR BEING THROUGH LIFE. HAPPILY, THERE IS A CORD WHICH TWISTED
AROUND THE ATONEMENT, OR BETTER STILL, AROUND THE PERSON OF
OUR LORD JESUS CHRIST, WHO IS OUR ONLY ALTAR, CAN HOLD US,
AND DOES HOLD US, "FOR THE LOVE OF CHRIST CONSTRAINS US."
——— C.H. SPURGEON

THIS IS AN ACROSTIC PSALM, DIVIDED INTO 22 STANZAS, ONE FOR EACH LETTER OF THE HEBREW ALPHABET. EACH VERSE OF EACH STANZA BEGINS WITH ONE OF THESE LETTERS.

PSALM 119

BLESSED ARE THE UNDEFILED IN THE WAY, WHO WALK IN THE LAW OF THE LORD.

BLESSED ARE THEY THAT KEEP HIS TESTIMONIES, AND THAT SEEK HIM WITH A WHOLE HEART.   VS. 1,2

HIS

LAW... A RULE OF CONDUCT PLACED CLEARLY IN MAN'S SIGHT, THEN ENFORCED BY A COMMAND.

TESTIMONIES... GODS OWN DECLARATIONS CONCERNING HIS NATURE AND PURPOSE.

PRECEPTS... RELATES TO MAN'S MORAL OBLIGATIONS AS ENJOINED BY GOD.

STATUTES... THAT MORAL LAW OF GOD WHICH IS ENGRAVEN ON THE FLESHLY TABLES OF THE HEART.

COMMANDMENTS... AUTHORITATIVE ORDERS USED AS RELIGIOUS PRINCIPLES.

JUDGEMENTS... LEGAL SANCTIONS, TO JUDGE OR DETERMINE.

ORDINANCES... LEGAL PRONOUNCEMENTS, RULES OF DIVINE ADMINISTRATION.

WORD... SAYING... THE ANNOUNCEMENT OF GODS REVEALED WILL.

WAY... THE ASSISTING GRACE OF GOD... THE PATHS OF LIFE MARKED OUT BY HIS LAW.

ESTHER

PSALM 119

WEREWITHALL SHALL A YOUNG MAN CLEANSE HIS WAY? BY TAKING HEED THERETO ACCORDING TO THY WORD.

Y.9

WITH THE GREATEST CARE A MAN WILL GO ASTRAY IF HIS MAP MISLEADS HIM, BUT WITH THE MOST ACCURATE MAP HE WILL STILL LOSE HIS ROAD IF HE DOES NOT TAKE HEED TO IT. THE NARROW WAY WAS NEVER HIT UPON BY CHANCE, NEITHER DID ANY HEEDLESS MAN EVER LEAD A HOLY LIFE. WE CAN SIN WITHOUT THOUGHT, WE HAVE ONLY TO NEGLECT THE GREAT SALVATION AND RUIN OUR SOULS; BUT TO OBEY THE LORD AND WALK UPRIGHTLY WILL NEED ALL OUR HEART AND SOUL AND MIND...

C.H. SPURGEON

THE WAY OF THE WORLD

HUMANISM

THE NEW AGE

BROADWAY

DEAD END

FOOLS WAY

MAP OF LIFE

INSTRU

GOD

LAW OF THE LORD

137

PSALM 119

ב Bĕth

I WILL MEDITATE IN THY PRECEPTS, AND HAVE RESPECT UNTO THY WAYS. I WILL DELIGHT MYSELF IN THY STATUTES; I WILL NOT FORGET THY WORD.

15-16

ג Gî´mel

DEAL BOUNTIFULLY WITH THY SERVANT, THAT I MAY LIVE, AND KEEP THY WORD. THY TESTIMONIES ALSO ARE MY DELIGHT AND MY COUNSELORS.

17,24

AND THE LORD SHALL GUIDE THEE CONTINUALLY, AND SATISFY THY SOUL IN DROUGHT, AND MAKE FAT THY BONES; AND THOU SHALT BE LIKE A WATERED GARDEN, AND LIKE A SPRING OF WATER, WHOSE WATERS FAIL NOT.

ISAIAH 58:11

PSALM 119

His soul cleaved to the dust; and it was not a casual and accidental falling into the dust, but a continuous and powerful tendency or cleaving to the earth....The serpent's seed can find their meat in the dust, but never shall the seed of the woman be thus degraded. Many are of the earth earthy and never lament it; only the heaven-born and heaven soaring spirit pines at the thought of being fastened to this world, and bird-limed by its sorrows or its pleasures.

His hope in his state of depression lies not in himself— but in his God... God strengthens us by infusing grace through His word. The word which creates can certainly sustain! Grace can enable us to bear the constant fret of an abiding sorrow, it can repair the decay caused by the perpetual tear-drip, and give to the believer the garment of praise for the spirit of heaviness.

C.H. SPURGEON

Earth-Bound!
MY SOUL CLEAVETH UNTO THE DUST; QUICKEN ME ACCORDING TO THY WORD.

MY SOUL MELTETH FOR HEAVINESS; STRENGTHEN THOU ME ACCORDING UNTO THY WORD.

VS. 25 & 28

PSALM 119

TEACH ME, O LORD, THE WAY OF THY STATUTES, AND I SHALL KEEP IT UNTO THE END.

GIVE ME UNDERSTANDING, AND I SHALL KEEP THY LAW; YEA, I SHALL OBSERVE IT WITH MY WHOLE HEART.

MAKE ME TO GO IN THE PATH OF THY COMMANDMENTS; FOR THEREIN DO I DELIGHT.   VS. 33-35

"IT IS A PLAIN PATH WHICH OTHERS ARE TREADING THROUGH THY GRACE; I SEE IT AND ADMIRE IT; CAUSE ME TO TRAVEL IN IT...THIS IS THE CRY OF A CHILD THAT LONGS TO WALK, BUT IS TOO FEEBLE; OF A PILGRIM WHO IS TOO EXHAUSTED, YET PANTS TO BE ON THE MARCH; OF A LAME MAN WHO PINES TO BE ABLE TO RUN.

IT IS A BLESSED THING TO DELIGHT IN HOLINESS, AND SURELY HE WHO GAVE US THIS DELIGHT WILL WORK IN US THE YET HIGHER JOY OF POSSESSING AND PRACTICING IT...MY SOLE DELIGHT LIES IN WALKING ACCORDING TO THY BIDDING."

— C.H. SPURGEON

PSALM 119

SO SHALL I KEEP THY LAW CONTINUALLY FOREVER AND EVER.

AND I WILL WALK AT LIBERTY; FOR I SEEK THY PRECEPTS.

I WILL SPEAK OF THY TESTIMONIES ALSO BEFORE KINGS, AND I WILL NOT BE ASHAMED.

AND I WILL DELIGHT MYSELF IN THY COMMANDMENTS, WHICH I HAVE LOVED.

MY HANDS ALSO WILL I LIFT UP UNTO THY COMMANDMENTS, WHICH I HAVE LOVED;

AND I WILL MEDITATE IN THY STATUTES.

44-48

GREAT PEACE HAVE THEY WHICH LOVE THY LAW;...
AND NOTHING SHALL OFFEND THEM.   V.165

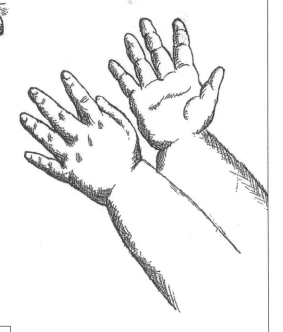

Where holy hands and hearts go,
the whole man will one day follow....
When mercy comes down, our hands
will be lifted up when
God in favour thinks upon us,
we are sure to think of him.
Happy is he who stands with hands
uplifted both to receive the blessing
and to obey the precept;
he shall not wait upon
the Lord in vain.   C.H. Spurgeon

PSALM 119

Horror hath taken hold upon me because of the wicked who forsake Thy law.

Thy statutes have been my songs in the house of my pilgrimage.

I have remembered Thy name, O Lord, in the night, and have kept Thy law.   53-55

The worldling clutches his money-bag and says, "This is my comfort"; the spendthrift points to his gaiety and shouts, "This is my comfort"; the drunkard lifts his glass and sings, "This is my comfort"; but the man whose hope comes from God feels the life-giving power of the Word of The Lord, and he testifies, "This is my comfort!"

Comfort is desirable at all times, but comfort in affliction is like a lamp in a dark place.

Blessed are the men whose "night-thoughts" are memories of eternal light. Are your thoughts in the dark full of light, because full of God? Then it will give a tone to your morning and noonday hours. Or do you give your whole mind to the fleeting cares & pleasures of this world? If so, it is little wonder that you do not live as you ought to do...No man is holy by chance...if you do not think of Him secretly you shall not obey Him openly.

— C.H. SPURGEON

PSALM 119

THOU ART MY PORTION, O LORD; I HAVE SAID THAT I WOULD KEEP THY WORDS. I ENTREATED THY FAVOR WITH MY WHOLE HEART; BE MERCIFUL UNTO ME ACCORDING TO THY WORD. I THOUGHT ON MY WAYS, AND TURNED MY FEET UNTO THY TESTIMONIES. I MADE HASTE AND DELAYED NOT TO KEEP THY COMMANDMENTS.   57-60

WHOM HAVE I IN HEAVEN BUT THEE?
AND THERE IS NONE UPON EARTH
THAT I DESIRE BESIDE THEE.
     MY FLESH AND MY HEART
FAILETH...BUT GOD IS THE
STRENGTH OF MY HEART,
AND MY PORTION FOREVER...
     BUT IT IS GOOD FOR ME
TO DRAW NEAR TO GOD;
I HAVE PUT MY TRUST
IN THE LORD GOD,
THAT I MAY DECLARE
ALL THY WORKS.
PSALM 73: 25, 26, 28

O CHRISTIAN, WHEN SATAN OR THE WORLD SHALL TEMPT THEE WITH HONOURS, ANSWER..."THE LORD IS MY PORTION"; AND WHEN THEY SHALL TEMPT THEE WITH RICHES, ANSWER..."THE LORD IS MY PORTION"; WHEN THEY SHALL TEMPT THEE WITH PREFERMENTS, ANSWER..."THE LORD IS MY PORTION"; AND WHEN THEY SHALL TEMPT THEE WITH FAVOURS OF GREAT ONES, ANSWER..."THE LORD IS MY PORTION"; YEA, AND WHEN THIS PERSECUTING WORLD SHALL THREATEN THEE WITH THE LOSS OF THY ESTATE, ANSWER..."THE LORD IS MY PORTION"; AND WHEN THEY SHALL THREATEN THEE WITH THE LOSS OF LIBERTY, ANSWER..."THE LORD IS MY PORTION"; AND WHEN THEY SHALL THREATEN THEE WITH LOSS OF LIFE, ANSWER............ ...."THE LORD IS MY PORTION!"
——— THOMAS BROOKS

PSALM 119

Before I was afflicted I went astray;...But now have I kept Thy word. Thou art good and doest good; teach me Thy statutes. It is good for me that I have been afflicted, that I might learn thy statues.   Vs. 67, 68, 71

Often our trials act as a thorn hedge to keep us in good pastures, but our prosperity is a gap through which we go astray....David would never have known and confessed his own strayings if he had not smarted under the rod. Even though the affliction came from bad men, it was overruled for good ends; though it was bad as it came from them it was good for David. ••• Whatever he may have thought under the trial, he perceived himself to be the better for it when it was over. C.H.Spurgeon

And when he had spent all, there arose a mighty famine in that land; and he began to be in want. And he went and joined himself to a citizen of that country; and he sent him into his fields to feed swine.

And he would fain have filled his belly with the husks that the swine did eat; and no man gave unto him.   Luke 15:14-16

144

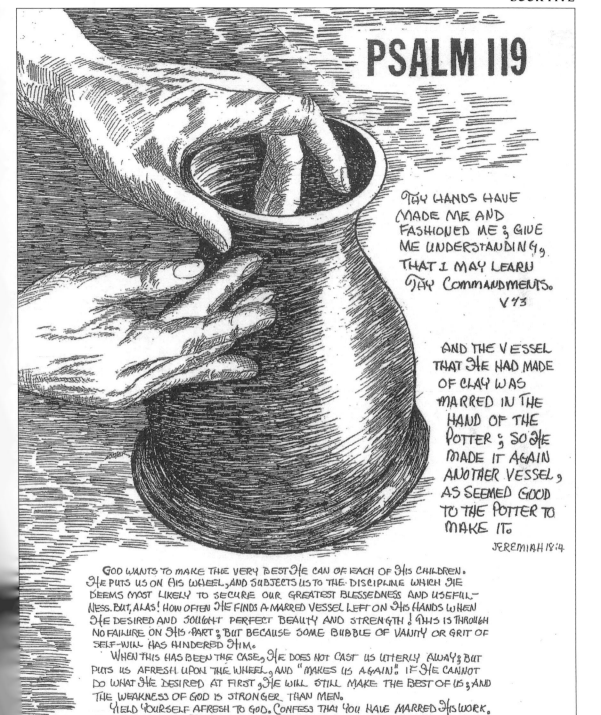

PSALM 119

THY HANDS HAVE MADE ME AND FASHIONED ME; GIVE ME UNDERSTANDING, THAT I MAY LEARN THY COMMANDMENTS.
V 73

AND THE VESSEL THAT HE HAD MADE OF CLAY WAS MARRED IN THE HAND OF THE POTTER; SO HE MADE IT AGAIN ANOTHER VESSEL, AS SEEMED GOOD TO THE POTTER TO MAKE IT.
JEREMIAH 18:4

GOD WANTS TO MAKE THE VERY BEST HE CAN OF EACH OF HIS CHILDREN. HE PUTS US ON HIS WHEEL, AND SUBJECTS US TO THE DISCIPLINE WHICH HE DEEMS MOST LIKELY TO SECURE OUR GREATEST BLESSEDNESS AND USEFULNESS. BUT, ALAS! HOW OFTEN HE FINDS A MARRED VESSEL LEFT ON HIS HANDS WHEN HE DESIRED AND SOUGHT PERFECT BEAUTY AND STRENGTH! THIS IS THROUGH NO FAILURE ON HIS PART; BUT BECAUSE SOME BUBBLE OF VANITY OR GRIT OF SELF-WILL HAS HINDERED HIM.

WHEN THIS HAS BEEN THE CASE, HE DOES NOT CAST US UTTERLY AWAY; BUT PUTS US AFRESH UPON THE WHEEL, AND "MAKES US AGAIN". IF HE CANNOT DO WHAT HE DESIRED AT FIRST, HE WILL STILL MAKE THE BEST OF US; AND THE WEAKNESS OF GOD IS STRONGER THAN MEN.

YIELD YOURSELF AFRESH TO GOD. CONFESS THAT YOU HAVE MARRED HIS WORK. HUMBLY ASK THAT HE SHOULD MAKE YOU AGAIN.... THERE IS SIMPLY NO LIMIT TO THE PROGRESS AND DEVELOPMENT OF THE SOUL WHICH IS ABLE TO MEET GOD WITH A NEVER-FALTERING "YES!"

F.B. MEYERS

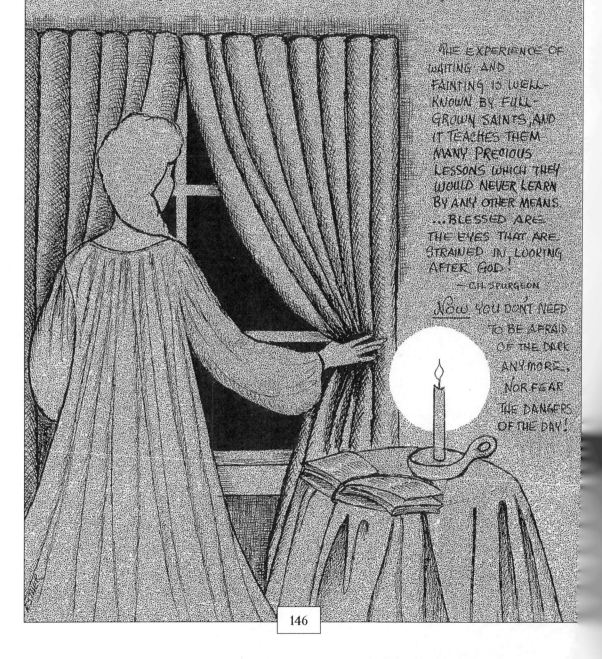

PSALM 119   OH, WHEN WILL MORNING COME?

MY SOUL FAINTETH FOR THY SALVATION, BUT I HOPE IN THY WORD. MINE EYES FAIL FOR THY WORD, SAYING, WHEN WILT THOU COMFORT ME?   V 81, 82

THE EXPERIENCE OF WAITING AND FAINTING IS WELL-KNOWN BY FULL-GROWN SAINTS, AND IT TEACHES THEM MANY PRECIOUS LESSONS WHICH THEY WOULD NEVER LEARN BY ANY OTHER MEANS. ...BLESSED ARE THE EYES THAT ARE STRAINED IN LOOKING AFTER GOD!
— C.H. SPURGEON

NOW YOU DON'T NEED TO BE AFRAID OF THE DARK ANYMORE, NOR FEAR THE DANGERS OF THE DAY!

146

PSALM 119

THE WORD

UNLESS THY LAW HAD BEEN MY DELIGHTS ... I SHOULD THEN HAVE PERISHED IN MINE AFFLICTION. V. 92

Forever, O Lord, thy word is settled in heaven. Thy faithfulness is unto all generations; thou hast established the earth, and it abideth. They continue this day according to thine ordinances; for all are thy servants...unless thy law had been my delight, I should have perished in mine affliction!
Psalm 119:89-92

"After tossing about on a sea of trouble the psalmist leaps to shore and stands upon a rock. Jehovah's word is not fickle or uncertain it is settled, determined, fixed, sure, immovable. Man's teaching change so often that there is never time for them to be settled. But the Lord's word is from old the same, and will remain unchanged eternally...He is not only faithful to one man throughout his lifetime, but to his children's children after him, yea, and to all generations so long as thy keep his covenant and remember his commandments to do them. The promises are ancient things, yet they are not worn out by centuries of use!" —C.H. Spurgeon

PSALM 119:102,103

"HOW SWEET ARE THY WORDS UNTO
MY TASTE! YEA, SWEETER THAN HONEY
TO MY MOUTH."
"WHEN HE (THE PSALMIST) DID NOT ONLY EAT
BUT ALSO SPOKE THE WORD, BY INSTRUCTING
OTHERS, HE FELT AN INCREASING DELIGHT IN IT.
THE SWEETEST OF ALL TEMPORAL THINGS FALL
SHORT OF THE INFININTE DELICIOUSNESS OF THE
ETERNAL WORD...HONEY ITSELF IS OUTSTRIPPED
IN SWEETNESS BY THE WORD OF THE LORD...
HOW WISE IT WILL BE ON OUR PART TO KEEP
THE WORD ON OUR PALATE BY MEDITATION
AND ON OUR TONGUE BY CONFESSION. IT
MUST BE SWEET TO OUR TASTE WHEN WE
THINK OF IT...OR IT WILL NOT BE SWEET TO
OUR MOUTH WHEN WE TALK OF IT."
C. H. SPURGEON

AND THE HOUSE OF ISRAEL
CALLED THE NAME THEREOF-MANNA:
AND IT WAS LIKE CORIANDER SEED,
WHITE, AND THE TASTE OF IT WAS
LIKE WAFERS MADE WITH HONEY.
EXODUS 16:31

I AM THE BREAD OF LIFE.
YOUR FATHERS DID EAT MANNA IN
THE WILDERNESS, AND ARE DEAD.
THIS IS THE BREAD THAT COMETH
DOWN FROM HEAVEN, THAT A MAN
MAY EAT OF IT, AND NOT DIE.
JESUS   JOHN 6: 48-50

THE WORD

THOU PREPAREST A TABLE BEFORE ME IN THE PRESENCE OF MINE ENEMIES!
PSALM 23:5

PSALM 119

IT IS TIME FOR THEE, LORD, TO WORK; FOR THEY HAVE MADE VOID THY LAW. THEREFORE, I LOVE THY COMMANDMENTS ABOVE GOLD; YEA, ABOVE FINE GOLD.

VS. 126, 127

MEN MAKE VOID THE LAW OF GOD BY DENYING IT TO BE HIS LAW, BY PROMULGATING COMMANDS AND DOCTRINES IN OPPOSITION TO IT, BY SETTING UP TRADITION IN ITS PLACE, OR BY UTTERLY DISREGARDING AND SCORNING THE AUTHORITY OF THE LAWGIVER. THEN SIN BECOMES FASHIONABLE, AND A HOLY WALK IS REGARDED AS A CONTEMPTIBLE PURITANISM; VICE IS STYLED PLEASURE, AND VANITY BEARS THE BELL. THEN THE SAINTS SIGH FOR THE PRESENCE AND POWER OF THEIR GOD: OH FOR AN HOUR OF THE KING UPON THE THRONE AND THE ROD OF IRON! OH FOR ANOTHER PENTECOST WITH ALL ITS WONDERS, TO REVEAL THE ENERGY OF GOD TO GAINSAYERS, AND MAKE THEM SEE THAT THERE IS A GOD IN ISRAEL! MAN'S EXTREMITY, WHETHER OF NEED OR SIN, IS GOD'S OPPORTUNITY. WHEN THE EARTH WAS WITHOUT FORM AND VOID, THE SPIRIT CAME AND MOVED UPON THE FACE OF THE WATERS; SHOULD HE NOT COME WHEN SOCIETY IS RETURNING TO LIKE CHAOS?

...HOW HEARTILY MAY WE PRAY THE LORD TO RAISE UP NEW EVANGELISTS, TO QUICKEN THOSE WE ALREADY HAVE, TO SET HIS CHURCH ON FIRE, AND TO BRING THE WORLD TO HIS FEET!

— CHS.

The ship is the symbol of the Church. In the third Century, Hippolytus wrote, "The world is a sea, in which the Church, like a ship, is beaten by the waves...but not submerged!"

PSALM 119

"Jesus, the Eternal Word, is called "Wonderful", and all the uttered words of God are wonderful in their degree — Those who know Him best ... wonder at them most."

Thy Testimonies are wonderful; therefore doth my soul keep them. The entrance of Thy words giveth light; it giveth understanding unto the simple. 129,130

Order my steps in Thy Word, and let not any iniquity have dominion over me. 133

Make Thy face to shine upon Thy servant, and teach me Thy statutes. 135

"The entrance of Thy words giveth light." No sooner do they gain admission into the soul than they enlighten it: what light may be expected from their prolonged indwelling! Their very entrance floods the mind with instructions, for they are so full, so clear; but on the other hand, there must be such an "entrance," or there will be no illumination. The mere hearing of the word with the external ear is of small value by itself, but when the words of God enter into the chambers of the heart then light is scattered on all sides. The word finds no entrance into some minds because they are blocked up with self-conceit, or prejudice, or indifference; but where due attention is given, divine illumination must surely follow upon knowledge of the mind of God.... Oh, that Thy words, like the beams of the sun, may enter through the window of my understanding and dispel the darkness of my mind! —C.H. SPURGEON

PSALM 119

YOUR WORD IS VERY PURE—TRIED AND WELL REFINED; THEREFORE YOUR SERVANT LOVES IT.

I AM SMALL (INSIGNIFICANT) AND DESPISED, BUT I DO NOT FORGET YOUR PRECEPTS.

YOUR RIGHTEOUSNESS IS AN EVERLASTING RIGHTEOUSNESS, AND YOUR LAW IS TRUTH.   140-142

Jesus loves me! This I know, for the Bible tells me so; Little ones to Him belong; They are weak ... but He is strong!

Yes, Jesus loves me, Yes, Jesus loves me, Yes, Jesus loves me ... The Bible tells me so!

PSALM 119

THY WORD IS VERY PURE: THEREFORE THY SERVANT LOUETH IT.
I AM SMALL AND DESPISED:YET DO NOT I FORGET THY PRECEPTS.
THE RIGHTEOUSNESS OF THY TESTIMONIES IS EVERLASTING:...
GIVE ME UNDERSTANDING, AND I SHALL LIVE.   VV 140,141,144

JESUS SAID —
"IF ANY MAN
THIRST — LET HIM
COME UNTO ME —
        AND
    DRINK !"
            JN. 7:37

HE TURNETH THE WILDERNESS
INTO A POOL OF WATER AND DRY
GROUND INTO WATER SPRINGS.
            PS.107:35

PSALM 119

I CRIED WITH MY WHOLE HEART, HEAR ME, O LORD; I WILL KEEP THY STATUES... I ANTICIPATED THE DAWNING OF THE MORNING, AND CRIED; I HOPED IN THY WORD. MINE EYES ANTICIPATE THE NIGHT WATCHES, THAT I MIGHT MEDITATE IN THY WORD... THOU ART NEAR, O LORD, AND ALL THY COMMANDMENTS ARE TRUTH.   145, 147, 148, 151

GOD LOOKS NOT AT THE ELEGANCY OF YOUR PRAYERS, TO SEE HOW NEAT THEY ARE; NOR YET AT THE GEOMETRY OF YOUR PRAYERS, TO SEE HOW LONG THEY ARE; NOR YET AT THE ARITHMETIC OF YOUR PRAYERS, TO SEE HOW MANY THEY ARE; NOR YET AT THE MUSIC OF YOUR PRAYERS, NOR YET AT THE SWEETNESS OF YOUR VOICE, NOR YET AT THE LOGIC OF YOUR PRAYERS, BUT AT THE SINCERITY OF YOUR PRAYERS, HOW HEARTY THEY ARE... PRAYER IS ONLY LOVELY AND WEIGHTY, AS THE HEART IS IN IT, AND NO OTHERWISE. IT IS NOT LIFTING UP OF THE VOICE, NOR THE WRINGING OF THE HANDS, NOR THE BEATING OF THE BREASTS, NOR AN AFFECTED TONE, NOR STUDIED MOTIONS, BUT THE STIRRINGS OF THE HEART, THAT GOD LOOKS AT IN PRAYER. GOD HEARS NO MORE THAN THE HEART SPEAKS.
— THOMAS BROOKS

EARLY PRAYERS ARE UNDISTURBED BY THE AGITATING CARES OF LIFE, AND RESEMBLE THE SWEET MELODY OF THOSE BIRDS WHICH SING LOUDEST AND SWEETEST WHEN FEWEST EARS ARE OPEN TO LISTEN TO THEM.... HAS THE DESIRE FOR COMMUNION WITH HEAVEN RAISED THEE FROM THY SLUMBERS, SHAKEN OFF THY SLOTH, AND CARRIED THEE TO THY KNEES?   — JOHN MORISON

Never see the face of man till you have first seen the face of God. — C.H.S.

LIFE!

CONSIDER HOW I LOVE THY PRECEPTS:
QUICKEN ME, O LORD, ACCORDING TO
THY LOVING KINDNESS.

PSALM 119:159

Breath on me, Breath of God,
Fill me with life anew.
That I may love what Thou dost love
And do what Thou wouldst do.

EDWIN HATCH 1835-1889

BENEATH THE SNOW OF INDIFFERENCE,
COVERED WITH THE ICE OF PAIN,
DORMANT LIES MY SOUL, O LORD,
QUICKEN ME ... AGAIN.

PSALM 119

I REJOICE IN YOUR LAWS LIKE ONE WHO FINDS A GREAT TREASURE.
HOW I HATE ALL FALSEHOOD. BUT HOW I LOVE
YOUR LAWS.   162, 163
     I HAVE LOOKED FOR YOUR COMMANDMENTS
AND I LOVE THEM VERY MUCH; YES, I
HAVE SEARCHED FOR THEM. YOU KNOW THIS
BECAUSE EVERYTHING I DO IS KNOWN
TO YOU.   167, 168

THE PSALMIST MAY HAVE REJOICED AS ONE WHO COMES UPON HIDDEN TREASURE FOR
WHICH HE HAD NOT FOUGHT, IN WHICH CASE WE FIND THE ANALOGY IN THE MAN OF GOD WHO,
WHILE READING THE BIBLE, MAKES GRAND AND BLESSED DISCOVERIES OF THE GRACE OF GOD
LAID UP FOR HIM,....DISCOVERIES WHICH SURPRISE HIM, FOR HE LOOKED NOT TO FIND SUCH A
PRIZE.....HOW GLAD SHOULD THAT MAN BE WHO HAS DISCOVERED HIS PORTION IN THE
PROMISES OF HOLY WRIT, AND IS ABLE TO ENJOY IT FOR HIMSELF, KNOWING BY THE WITNESS
OF THE HOLY SPIRIT THAT IT IS ALL HIS OWN!   -C. H. SPURGEON

PSALM 119

LET MY CRY COME NEAR BEFORE THEE, O LORD; GIVE ME UNDERSTANDING ACCORDING TO THY WORD.

I HAVE GONE ASTRAY LIKE A LOST SHEEP; SEEK THY SERVANT; FOR I DO NOT FORGET THY COMMANDMENTS.   VS. 169, 176

SAFE WERE THE NINETY AND NINE IN THE FOLD,
   SAFE THOUGH THE NIGHT WAS STORMY AND COLD;
BUT SAID THE SHEPHERD, WHEN COUNTING THEM O'ER,
   "ONE SHEEP IS MISSING; THERE SHOULD BE ONE MORE!"
ALTHOUGH HIS FEET WERE WEARY AND WORN,
   AND THOUGH HIS HANDS WERE RENT AND TORN;
E'EN THO' THE ROAD WAS RUGGED AND STEEP,
   STILL THE GOOD SHEPHERD SOUGHT LONG FOR HIS SHEEP.
THERE IN THE NIGHT HE HEARD A FAINT CRY
   FROM THE LOST SHEEP JUST READY TO DIE;
THEN IN HIS ARMS, TO SHIELD FROM THE COLD,
   HE BROUGHT THE LOST ONE SAFE BACK TO THE FOLD.
THE SHEPHERD WENT OUT TO SEARCH FOR HIS SHEEP, AND ALL THRO' THE NIGHT ON THE ROCKY STEEP HE SOUGHT TILL HE FOUND HIM, WITH LOVE-BANDS HE BOUND HIM...
...AND I WAS THAT ONE LOST SHEEP.   — L. PHILLIP KNOX

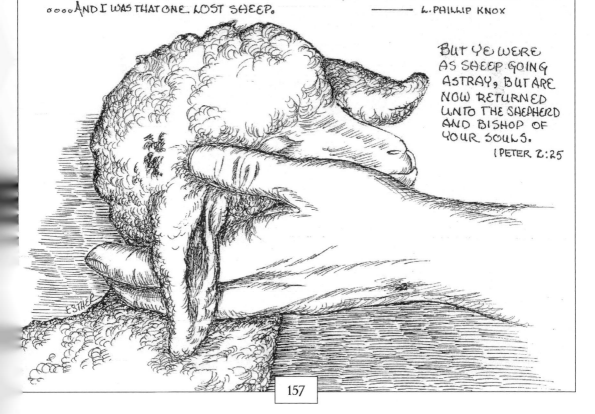

BUT YE WERE AS SHEEP GOING ASTRAY, BUT ARE NOW RETURNED UNTO THE SHEPHERD AND BISHOP OF YOUR SOULS.
I PETER 2:25

157

IN MY DISTRESS I CRIED UNTO LORD
...AND HE HEARD ME. V 1

IN ALL WAYS IT IS A SORE
DISTRESS TO COME UNDER THE POWER OF
SLANDER, THE FOULEST WHELP OF SIN.
SILENCE TO MAN AND PRAYER TO GOD
ARE THE BEST CURES FOR THE EVIL OF
SLANDER. IT IS OF LITTLE USE TO APPEAL TO
OUR FELLOWS ON THE MATTER, FOR THE MORE
WE STIR IN IT THE MORE IT SPREADS; IT IS OF
NO AVAIL TO APPEAL TO THE HONOUR OF OUR
SLANDERERS, FOR THEY HAVE NONE... AS WELL
PLEAD WITH PANTHERS AND WOLVES AS WITH
BLACK-HEARTED TRADUCERS. HOWEVER, WHEN
CRIES TO MAN WOULD BE OUR WEAKNESS,
CRIES TO GOD WILL BE OUR STRENGTH.
    TO WHOM SHOULD CHILDREN CRY BUT TO
THEIR FATHER? DOES NOT SOME GOOD
COME EVEN OUT OF THAT VILE THING,
FALSEHOOD, WHEN IT DRIVES US TO
    OUR KNEES AND TO OUR GOD?
    YES, JEHOVAH HEARS!

    — SAMUEL COX

PSALM 120

158

Psalm 121
My KEEPER

BEHOLD, HE WHO KEEPETH ISRAEL SHALL NEITHER SLUMBER NOR SLEEP. THE LORD IS THY KEEPER: THE LORD IS THY SHADE UPON THY RIGHT HAND THE SUN SHALL NOT SMITE THEE BY DAY NOR THE MOON BY NIGHT. vv 4-6

"The Lord is thy keeper." The emphasis of the psalm as a whole is upon the fact that our security is the Lord's responsibility. We do not have to struggle to keep ourselves saved. The sheep never trouble themselves about keeping the shepherd. That the Lord is well able to keep His own is evidenced by two of His characteristic features-he made heaven and earth; and He neither slumbers nor sleeps.
--H.Lockyer

PSALM 122

Pray for the peace of Jerusalem; they shall prosper who love thee. Peace be within thy walls, and prosperity within thy palaces.
VV 6, 7

What the earthly Jerusalem was to the Jews, that the Holy Church, the Bride of The Lamb, the Heavenly Jerusalem, which descends from God out of Heaven, and includes within its limits all holy souls, is to us. Let us pray for its peace and prosperity. Let us esteem them above our own good, and let us be glad if our feet stand within its gates.

Let us ascend the staircases of prayer and praise; let us mingle our rivulet of adoring love in the mighty torrent that is setting in towards the Throne of God and The Lamb.

F.B. MEYER

ℑsalm 123

*Unto thee lift I up mine eyes, O thou that dwellest in the heavens. Behold, as the eyes of servants look unto the hand of their masters, and as the eyes of a maiden unto the hand of her mistress; so our eyes wait upon the Lord our God, **until** that he have mercy upon us. vv. 1, 2*

THE SLAVE AT THE TABLE KEPT THE EYE STEADFASTLY FIXED ON THE HAND OF MASTER OR MISTRESS TO OBEY ITS LEAST SIGN AND TO MAKE IT NEEDLESS TO SPEAK. KEEP YOUR EYE ON THE PIERCED HAND, CHILD OF GOD; WATCH ITS SMALLEST INDICATION WAIT PATIENTLY **UNTIL** IT GAVE SOME SIGN. WE HAVE TOO LONG ACTED ON OUR OWN INITIATIVE; LET US WAIT ON OUR EXALTED LORD FOR THE INDICATION OF HIS WILL.

ONE DAY WE SHALL FOLLOW THE DIRECTION OF OUR EYES. WHILST WE GAZE, WE SHALL BE CHANGED; AND AS WE ARE CHANGED WE SHALL ARISE TO SIT WITH HIM ON HIS THRONE.

—F.B. MEYER

"Until Then"
"My heart can sing when I pause to remember,
A heartache here is but a stepping stone
Along a trail that's winding always upwards,
This troubled world is not my final home.

The things of earth will dim and lose their value,
If we recall they're borrowed for a while,
And things of earth that cause the heart to tremble,
Remembered there will only bring a smile.

This weary world with all it's toil and struggle,
May take its toll of misery and strife
The soul of man is like a waiting falcon,
When it's released it's destined for the skies.

But, until then my heart will go on singing,
Until then with joy I'll carry on,
Until the day my eyes behold the city,
Until the day God calls me home."
-Stuart Hamblen

PSALM 124

Our soul is escaped like a bird out
of the snare of the fowlers; the snare is
broken and we are escaped!
Our help is in the Name of the Lord,
who made Heaven and Earth.   vs. 7, 8

Lo, floods of wrath, and floods of hell,
In fierce impetuous torrents roll;
Had not the Lord defended well,
The waters had o'erwhelmed my soul.

As when the fowler's snare is broke,
The bird escapes on cheerful wings;
My soul, set free from Satan's yoke,
With joy bursts forth, and mounts and sings.

She sings the Lord her Saviour's praise;
Sings forth His praise with joy and mirth;
To Him her song in heaven she'll raise,
To Him that made both Heaven and Earth.
— C.H. Spurgeon

O for a thousand tongues to sing
My great Redeemer's praise,
The glories of my God and King,
The triumphs of His grace!

He breaks the power of canceled sin,
He sets the prisoner free;
His blood can make the foulest clean,
His blood availed for me.
— Charles Wesley

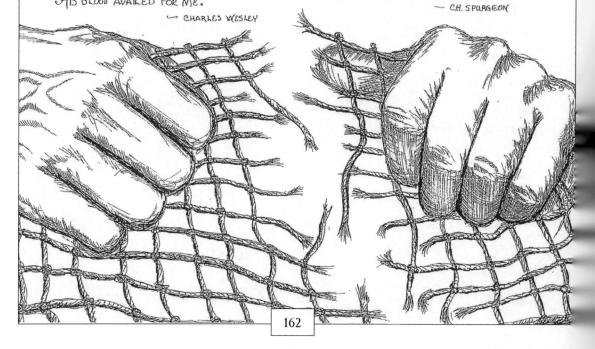

PSALM 125

AS THE MOUNTAINS ARE ROUND ABOUT JERUSALEM, SO THE LORD IS ROUND ABOUT HIS PEOPLE FROM HENCEFORTH EVEN FOREVER.   V.2

I WILL BE UNTO HER A WALL OF FIRE ROUND ABOUT AND THE GLORY IN THE MIDST OF HER.   ZECH. 2:5

AROUND THE CHOSEN CITY THE MOUNTAINS STOOD LIKE SENTINALS. SO IS GOD AROUND US; AND THIS ENABLES US TO UNDERSTAND HOW HIS PERMISSIONS MAY BECOME HIS APPOINTMENTS... THIS WILL BECOME EVIDENT, IF WE CLEARLY APPREHEND THAT GOD IS ROUND ABOUT US AS A RAMPART TO THE CITY ...AS AN ENVELOPE TO A LETTER.... AS THE ATMOSPHERE TO THE CONFIGURATION OF OUR BODIES. IF THEN HE CHOOSES, HE CAN PASS OFF FROM US ANY ARROW THAT MIGHT HARM US; BUT IF HE OPENS HIS ENVIRONING PROTECTION,

SO AS TO LET IT PASS THROUGH TO US, BY THE TIME IT HAS TRAVERSED THE ATMOSPHERE OF HIS CARE, IT HAS BECOME HIS WILL FOR US.... PUT GOD BETWEEN YOURSELF AND EVERYTHING! MANY PUT THEIR ANXIETIES BETWEEN THEM AND GOD, AND SEE GOD AS THE SUN THROUGH A FOG; MIND THAT YOU PUT GOD BETWEEN YOURSELF AND THE ENTIRE WORLD OF MEN AND THINGS.
— F.B. MEYER

They that sow in tears shall reap in joy. He that goeth forth and weepeth, bearing precious seed, shall doubtless come again with rejoicing, bringing his sheaves with him. Vs. 5, 6

PSALM 126

What a promise is here! You have sown long and patiently among young or old, sometime to the point of giving all up in despair; but to give up now would be to miss the harvest and reward of all your toils. Be patient, persevere a little longer. God guarantees the harvest. Even though you were to die without reaping, yet in another world you would come again, bringing your sheaves.

We are all sowing tears—tears over our darling Absaloms, tears over our failures and mistakes, tears over our disappointed hopes. But each tear overflowing from a consecrated soul is a seed-germ dropped into God's keeping, and it shall have its reward. He carefully gathers up our tears for his bottle. God is not unrighteous to forget. He guards the buried seed and stands sponsor for the harvest. No sigh, no tear, no prayer, inspired by the Spirit of God can positively be lost or unproductive. —F.B. Meyer

LO, CHILDREN ARE AN HERITAGE OF THE LORD: AND THE FRUIT OF THE WOMB IS HIS REWARD. V3

PSALM 127

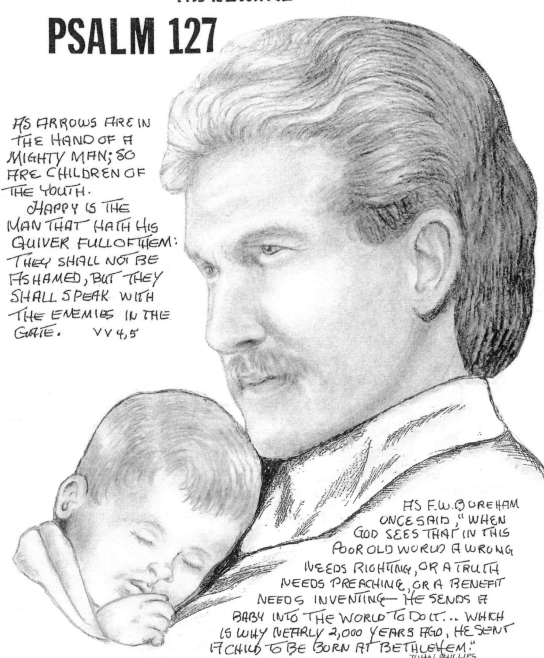

AS ARROWS ARE IN THE HAND OF A MIGHTY MAN; SO ARE CHILDREN OF THE YOUTH.

HAPPY IS THE MAN THAT HATH HIS QUIVER FULL OF THEM: THEY SHALL NOT BE ASHAMED, BUT THEY SHALL SPEAK WITH THE ENEMIES IN THE GATE. VV 4,5

AS F.W. BOREHAM ONCE SAID, "WHEN GOD SEES THAT IN THIS POOR OLD WORLD A WRONG NEEDS RIGHTING, OR A TRUTH NEEDS PREACHING, OR A BENEFIT NEEDS INVENTING — HE SENDS A BABY INTO THE WORLD TO DO IT... WHICH IS WHY NEARLY 2,000 YEARS AGO, HE SENT A CHILD TO BE BORN AT BETHLEHEM."
— JOHN PHILLIPS

The Blessing

BLESSED IS EVERYONE THAT FEARETH THE LORD; THAT WALKETH IN HIS WAYS. FOR THOU SHALT EAT THE LABOUR OF THINE HANDS; HAPPY SHALT THOU BE, AND IT SHALL BE WELL WITH THEE. THY WIFE SHALL BE A FRUITFUL VINE BY THE SIDE OF THINE HOUSE; THY CHILDREN LIKE OLIVE PLANTS ROUND ABOUT THY TABLE ... BEHOLD ... THAT THUS SHALL THE MAN BE BLESSED THAT FEARETH THE LORD. V. 1-4

Psalm 128

Psalm 129

IN THE DEN .... AGAIN.

MANY A TIME HAVE THEY AFFLICTED ME FROM MY YOUTH, MAY ISRAEL NOW SAY, MANY A TIME HAVE THEY AFFLICTED ME FROM MY YOUTH; YET THEY HAVE NOT PREVAILED AGAINST ME! VV. 1,2.

FOR OUR LIGHT AFFLICTION, WHICH IS BUT FOR A MOMENT, WORKETH FOR US A FAR MORE EXCEEDING AND ETERNAL WEIGHT OF GLORY. 2 CORINTHIANS 4:17

WHAT A WONDER IT IS THAT SATAN AND MAN DO NOT PREVAIL AGAINST THE SAINT! THERE IS NO WAY OF ACCOUNTING FOR IT, EXCEPT IN GOD'S ELECTION. BECAUSE GOD HAS CHOSEN US FOR HIMSELF, AND REDEEMED US AT GREAT COST, HE CANNOT AFFORD TO HAND US OVER TO THE WILL OF OUR ENEMIES. HE MAY ALLOW OUR BACKS TO BE FURROWED BY THE HEAVY SCOURGE, BECAUSE THE SERVANT MUST BE AS HIS LORD; BUT HE WILL CUT OUR CORDS IN THE DAY SELECTED FOR OUR EXECUTION. .... LET US THEN WALK WITH GOD. IF WE CULTIVATE THE FRESH SENSE OF FELLOWSHIP WITH HIM, WE SHALL NOT YIELD TO FEAR, BE OUR FOES NEVER SO VENOMOUS AND THEIR PLANS NEVER SO INSIDIOUS. A CLOSE WALK WITH GOD IS THE SURE WAY OF ESCAPING THEM!

— F.B. MEYER

PSALM 130

I'M DEPENDING ON YOU, OH LORD!!

OUT OF THE DEPTHS HAVE I CRIED UNTO THEE, O LORD
V.1

PSALM 131

SPIRIT OF GOD,
DESCEND UPON MY HEART

Spirit of God, descend upon my heart;
Wean it from earth; through all its pulses move;
Stoop to my weakness, mighty as Thou art,
And make me love Thee as I ought to love.

I ask no dream, no prophet ecstasies,
No sudden rending of the veil of clay,
No angel visitant, no opening skies;
But take the dimness of my soul away. G. Croly

LORD, MY HEART IS NOT HAUGHTY, NOR MINE EYES LOFTY; NEITHER DO I EXERCISE MYSELF IN GREAT MATTERS, OR IN THINGS TOO HIGH FOR ME.

SURELY, I HAVE BEHAVED AND QUIETED MYSELF, LIKE A CHILD THAT IS WEANED OF HIS MOTHER; MY SOUL IS EVEN LIKE A WEANED CHILD.   VS. 1, 2

PSALM 132

FOR THE LORD HATH CHOSEN ZION; HE HATH DESIRED IT FOR HIS HABITATION. THIS IS MY REST FOREVER; HERE WILL I DWELL; FOR I HAVE DESIRED IT. I WILL ABUNDANTLY BLESS HER PROVISION; I WILL SATISFY HER POOR WITH BREAD. I WILL CLOTHE HER PRIESTS WITH SALVATION; AND HER SAINTS SHALL SHOUT ALOUD FOR JOY!   VV. 13-16

God in His church is the wonder of
heaven, the miracle of eternity, the glory of infinite love! C.H. Spurgeon

WHAT?
KNOW YE NOT
THAT YOUR BODY
IS THE TEMPLE
OF THE HOLY
GHOST WHICH IS
IN YOU — WHICH
YE HAVE OF GOD
AND —
YE ARE NOT
YOUR OWN?   1 COR. 6:19

Shekinah

PSALM 133

BEHOLD, HOW GOOD AND HOW PLEASANT IT IS FOR BRETHREN TO DWELL TOGETHER IN UNITY! IT IS LIKE THE PRECIOUS OINTMENT UPON THE HEAD, THAT RAN DOWN UPON THE BEARD, EVEN AARON'S BEARD: THAT WENT DOWN TO THE SKIRTS OF HIS GARMENTS. LIKE THE DEW OF HERMON, AND LIKE THE DEW THAT DESCENDED UPON THE MOUNTAINS OF ZION... V.V. 1-3

BELOVED, IF GOD SO LOVED US, WE OUGHT TO LOVE ONE ANOTHER.
— 1 JOHN 4:11

BROTHERLY LOVE BINDING TOGETHER KINDRED HEARTS IS HERE COMPARED TO OIL, THE CHOSEN SYMBOL OF THE HOLY SPIRIT, BECAUSE IT IS ONLY THROUGH HIS GRACE THAT IT IS POSSIBLE TO LOVE. THE LOVE OF THE BRETHREN IS THE EARTHLY MANIFESTATION OF LOVE TO GOD. WE HAVE JUST AS MUCH TO HIM AS WE HAVE TO THEM.... THE HOLY SPIRIT AS OIL, WAS POURED UPON THE HEAD OF OUR GREAT AARON AS HE AROSE FROM THE WATERS OF BAPTISM, AND AGAIN WHEN HE ASCENDED INTO THE PRESENCE OF HIS FATHER; AND IT HAS BEEN DESCENDING EVER SINCE UPON US WHO ARE THE SKIRTS OF HIS GARMENTS .... THUS, FROM THE GLORY OF HIS EXALTATION, JESUS DROPS THE DEW OF THE HOLY SPIRIT AS BLESSING UPON THE LOWLANDS OF OUR LIFE — THAT BLESSING WHICH IS LIFE FOR EVERMORE. — F.B. MEYER

BROTHERLY LOVE IS ESSENTIAL TO THE NATURE AND WELFARE OF THE CHURCH. IT IS A SYMPATHY ACTUATED BY A SENSE OF COMMUNION IN THE SAME HOPES, THE SAME FEARS, THE SAME AVERSIONS AND IN THE BENEVOLENCE OF THE SAME PARENT.
— WILLIAM NICHOLSON

PSALM 134

BEHOLD, BLESS YE THE LORD, ALL YE SERVANTS OF THE LORD, WHO BY NIGHT STAND IN THE HOUSE OF THE LORD. LIFT UP YOUR HANDS IN THE SANCTUARY, AND BLESS THE LORD.
Vs. 1,2

IT IS TO BE NOTICED THAT THESE WERE ESPECIALLY SUMMONED TO BLESS THE LORD AND LIFT UP THEIR HANDS. FOR, AFTER ALL, IS IT NOT THEY THAT STAND IN THE HOUSE OF GOD BY NIGHT WHO ARE MOST IN NEED OF THESE EXHORTATIONS? IT SEEMS TO US THAT THE SLEEPLESS SUFFERERS AMONG US ARE GOD'S NIGHT-WATCH. WHEN THE BUSY WORKERS ARE SLUMBERING, THEY COME ON DUTY TO BLESS THE LORD.

IT IS COMPARATIVELY EASY TO BLESS THE LORD IN THE DAYTIME, WHEN SUNSHINE LIES LIKE HIS SMILE ON NATURE, AND ALL THE WORLD IS FULL OF MUSIC, AND OUR LIVES FLOW ON QUIETLY AND PEACEFULLY, IT DOES NOT TAKE MUCH GRACE TO BLESS THE LORD, THEN. BUT WHEN NIGHT HAS DRAPED THE EARTH AND HUSHED THE HOMES OF MEN IN SOLITUDE, AND WE STAND AMID THE SHADOWS THAT LURK AROUND US IN THE SANCTUARY, FACING THE INEXPLICABLE MYSTERIES OF PROVIDENCE, OF HISTORY, OF LIFE AND DEATH, THEN THE SONG FALTERS ON OUR LIPS, AND CHOKES OUR UTTERANCE.

NO SOONER, HOWEVER, DO WE DARE TO FORMULATE THE WORDS OF BLESSING, PURSING OUR LIPS IN THE EFFORT, DARING TO SAY, BY THE STRONG EFFORT OF WILL, WHAT WE MAY NOT SAY GLADLY AND EASILY, THERE COMES BACK TO US, AS TO THIS ANCIENT SINGER, THE ASSURANCE THAT THE LORD WHICH MADE HEAVEN AND EARTH SHALL BLESS. IS IT POSSIBLE FOR HIM TO HAVE MADE HEAVEN AND EARTH, AND NOT BE ABLE TO BLESS THE SOUL WHOM HE HAS NOT CREATED ONLY, BUT REDEEMED! HE CANNOT FAIL TO BLESS THOSE THAT BLESS.

— F.B. MEYER

I WILL BLESS THE LORD, AT ALL TIMES, HIS PRAISE SHALL CONTINUALLY, BE IN MY MOUTH!

PSALM 34:1

PSALM 135

PRAISE YE THE LORD. PRAISE YE THE NAME OF THE LORD; PRAISE HIM, O YE SERVANTS OF THE LORD! V.1
IF OTHERS ARE SILENT, YOU MUST NOT BE; YOU MUST BE FIRST TO CELEBRATE HIS PRAISES. YOU ARE SERVANTS, AND
THIS IS PART OF YOUR SERVICE; HIS NAME IS NAMED UPON YOU, THEREFORE CELEBRATE HIS NAME WITH PRAISES;
YOU KNOW WHAT A BLESSED MASTER HE IS, THEREFORE SPEAK WELL OF HIM. THOSE WHO SHUN HIS SERVICE ARE SURE
TO NEGLECT HIS PRAISE; BUT AS GRACE HAS MADE YOU HIS OWN PERSONAL SERVANTS, LET YOUR HEARTS MAKE YOU
HIS COURT-MUSICIANS.
                                                                    —C.H. SPURGEON

PSALM 136

OH, GIVE THANKS UNTO THE LORD FOR HE IS GOOD; FOR HIS MERCY ENDURETH FOREVER.

There's a wideness in God's mercy, like the wideness of the sea;
There's a kindness in His justice, which is more than liberty.
There's no place where earth's sorrows are more felt than up in heaven.
There is no place where earth's failings have such kindly judgement given.
For the love of God is broader than the measures of man's mind;
And the heart of the Eternal is more wonderfully kind.
If our love were but more simple, we should take Him at His word;
And our lives would be all sunshine in the sweetness of our Lord.

— D. WAGNER

PSALM 137

BY THE RIVERS OF BABYLON THERE WE
SAT DOWN... YEA, WE WEPT WHEN WE
REMEMBERED ZION.
WE HANGED OUR HARPS UPON THE
WILLOWS IN THE MIDST THEREOF.   VV 1,2

YOU HAVE CEASED SINGING LATELY. THE JOY OF
YOUR RELIGIOUS LIFE HAS VANISHED. YOU PASS THROUGH THE OLD
ROUTINE, BUT WITHOUT THE EXHILARATION OF FORMER DAYS.
CAN YOU NOT TELL THE REASON? IT IS NOT BECAUSE YOUR CIRCUMSTANCES
ARE DEPRESSED, THOUGH THEY MAY BE; FOR PAUL AND SILAS SANG
PRAISES TO GOD IN THEIR PRISON. IS NOT DISOBEDIENCE AT THE
ROOT OF YOUR SONGLESSNESS? YOU HAVE ALLOWED SOME LITTLE
RIFT TO COME WITHIN THE LUTE OF YOUR LIFE, WHICH HAS BEEN
SLOWLY WIDENING, AND NOW THREATENS TO SILENCE ALL. AND
YOU NEVER WILL BE ABLE TO RESUME THAT SONG UNTIL YOU HAVE
PUT AWAY THE EVIL OF YOUR DOING, AND HAVE RETURNED FROM
THE LAND OF THE ENEMY.

THE RETURN FROM BABYLON HAS ITS DUPLICATE IN
MANY A LIFE. IN ANSWER TO PRAYER OUR CAPTIVITY IS TURNED
AGAIN AS THE STREAM FROM THE SOUTH. DELIVERED OUT OF
THE LAND OF STRANGERS, WE AGAIN TAKE UP THE HARP OF PRAISE.
"THE LORD'S SONG" IS OFTEN MORE IN THE HEART THAN ON THE
LIPS. REMEMBER JONATHAN EDWARDS' DESCRIPTION OF THE
LADY WHO BECAME HIS WIFE, "WHOSE MIND WAS FILLED WITH
EXCEEDING SWEET DELIGHT AND SEEMED TO HAVE SOMEONE
INVISIBLE ALWAYS COMMUNING WITH HER."
— F.B. MEYER

175

I WILL PRAISE THEE WITH MY WHOLE HEART BEFORE THE gods WILL I SING PRAISE UNTO THEE.
THOUGH THE LORD BE HIGH YET HATH HE RESPECT UNTO THE LOWLY. BUT THE PROUD HE KNOWETH AFAR OFF. VV 1,6

...FOR THOU ART WITH ME; THY ROD AND THY STAFF THEY COMFORT ME!
PSALM 23:4

THOUGH I WALK IN THE MIDST OF TROUBLE THOU WILT REVIVE ME THOU SHALT STRETCH FORTH THINE HAND AGAINST THE WRATH OF MINE ENEMIES AND THY RIGHT HAND SHALL SAVE ME. V 7

PSALM 138

PSALM 139

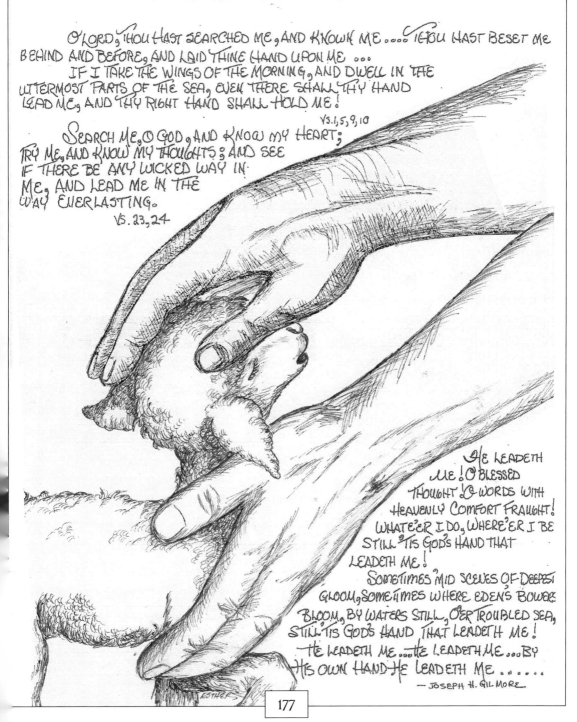

O LORD, THOU HAST SEARCHED ME, AND KNOWN ME.... THOU HAST BESET ME BEHIND AND BEFORE, AND LAID THINE HAND UPON ME ...

IF I TAKE THE WINGS OF THE MORNING, AND DWELL IN THE UTTERMOST PARTS OF THE SEA, EVEN THERE SHALL THY HAND LEAD ME, AND THY RIGHT HAND SHALL HOLD ME!

VS. 1, 5, 9, 10

SEARCH ME, O GOD, AND KNOW MY HEART; TRY ME, AND KNOW MY THOUGHTS; AND SEE IF THERE BE ANY WICKED WAY IN ME, AND LEAD ME IN THE WAY EVERLASTING.

VS. 23, 24

HE LEADETH ME! O BLESSED THOUGHT! O WORDS WITH HEAVENLY COMFORT FRAUGHT! WHATE'ER I DO, WHERE'ER I BE STILL 'TIS GOD'S HAND THAT LEADETH ME!

SOMETIMES 'MID SCENES OF DEEPEST GLOOM, SOMETIMES WHERE EDEN'S BOWERS BLOOM, BY WATERS STILL, O'ER TROUBLED SEA, STILL 'TIS GOD'S HAND THAT LEADETH ME! HE LEADETH ME... HE LEADETH ME... BY HIS OWN HAND HE LEADETH ME ....

— JOSEPH H. GILMORE

ESTHER

PSALM 140

DELIVER ME, O LORD, FROM THE EVIL MAN, AND PRESERVE ME FROM THE VIOLENT MAN... O GOD, THE LORD, THE STRENGTH OF MY SALVATION, THOU HAST COVERED MY HEAD IN THE DAY OF BATTLE.   VS. 1, 7

GO YOUR WAYS; BEHOLD, I SEND YOU FORTH AS LAMBS AMONG WOLVES.
                                                    LUKE 10:3

AH, BELOVED SOUL, GOD IS NOT ONLY THE STRENGTH OF THY SALVATION, BUT HE IS ALSO THE COVERT, THE PANOPLY, THE SHIELD ON WHICH THE MALICE OF THE FOE EXPENDS ITSELF IN VAIN. BE QUIET... LET NOT YOUR HEART BE TROUBLED, NEITHER LET IT BE AFRAID. NO WEAPON THAT IS FORMED AGAINST THEE SHALL PROSPER... GOD'S COVERING IN THE DAY OF BATTLE MAKES A TEMPLE AMID ITS TUMULT, AND THE SOUL DWELLS THERE AS IN THE DIVINE PRESENCE CHAMBER.
                                                    — F.B. MEYER

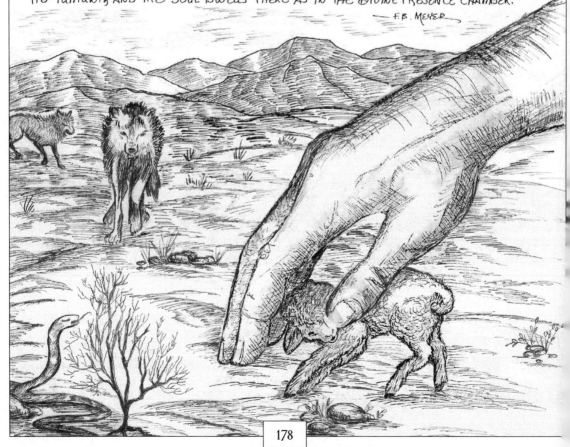

PSALM 141

LET MY PRAYER BE SET FORTH BEFORE THEE AS INCENSE; AND THE LIFTING UP OF MY HANDS, AS THE EVENING SACRIFICE. SET A WATCH, O LORD, BEFORE MY MOUTH; KEEP THE DOOR OF MY LIPS.

VS. 2, 3

KEEP THE DOOR OF MY LIPS, THAT IT MOVE NOT CREAKING AND COMPLAINING, AS ON RUSTY HINGES, FOR WANT OF THE OIL OF JOY AND GLADNESS.
— JOHN TRAPP

IF ANY MAN OFFEND NOT IN WORD, THE SAME IS A PERFECT MAN, AND IS ABLE, ALSO TO BRIDLE THE WHOLE BODY!
— JAMES 3:2

THAT MOUTH HAD BEEN USED IN PRAYER, IT WOULD BE A PITY IT SHOULD EVER BE DEFILED WITH UNTRUTH, OR PRIDE, OR WRATH; YET SO IT WILL BECOME UNLESS CAREFULLY WATCHED, FOR THESE INTRUDERS ARE EVER LURKING ABOUT THE DOOR... WHEN JEHOVAH SETS THE WATCH THE CITY IS WELL GUARDED; WHEN THE LORD BECOMES THE GUARD OF OUR MOUTH THE WHOLE MAN IS WELL GARRISONED... GOD HAS MADE OUR LIPS THE DOOR OF THE MOUTH, BUT WE CANNOT KEEP THAT DOOR OF OURSELVES, THEREFORE, DO WE ENTREAT THE LORD TO TAKE THE RULE OF IT. O THAT THE LORD WOULD BOTH OPEN AND SHUT OUR LIPS, FOR WE CAN DO NEITHER THE ONE NOR THE OTHER ARIGHT IF LEFT TO OURSELVES. IN TIME OF PERSECUTION BY UNGODLY MEN WE ARE PECULIARLY LIABLE TO SPEAK HASTILY, OR EVASIVELY, AND THEREFORE WE SHOULD BE SPECIALLY ANXIOUS TO BE PRESERVED IN THAT DIRECTION FROM EVERY FORM OF SIN.
— C. H. SPURGEON

PSALM 142
· "THE CAVE"

WHEN MY SPIRIT WAS OVERWHELMED WITHIN ME, THEN THOU KNEWEST MY PATH. IN THE WAY WHEREIN I WALKED HAVE THEY SECRETLY LAID A SNARE FOR ME... BRING MY SOUL OUT OF PRISON THAT I MAY PRAISE THY NAME.   V3,7

WE ALL HAVE OUR TIMES OF BEING OVERWHELMED WHEN THE FULL REALIZATION OF OUR GRIEF AND PAIN AND LONELINESS RUSHES OVER US. THE LOVE WE CAN NEVER RETRIEVE, THE OPPORTUNITY WE CAN NEVER RECALL. THEN THERE IS HEART-BREAK. BUT IN SUCH DARK HOURS JESUS KNOWS — KNOWS THE DIFFICULTIES YOU CANNOT EXPLAIN TO THE DEAREST, THE GRAVE PERPLEXITIES WHICH YOU CANNOT SHARE WITH YOUR WISEST CONFIDANT. HE CAN ALLOW FOR A HESITANCE, A TREPIDATION, A SHRINKING BACK, WHICH TO OTHERS ARE UNACCOUNTABLE. HE CAN GIVE CREDIT FOR THE RESOLUTION THAT IS SORELY TESTED, AND THE FAITH WHICH NEARLY GIVES OUT. HE CAN TAKE INTO ACCOUNT MATTERS WHICH EVADE THE SCRUTINY OF THOSE WHO HAVE THE BEST OPPORTUNITY OF JUDGING.
WHAT A RELIEF TO TURN FROM THEM TO HIM, AND SAY... ...I CANNOT TELL THEM... BUT THOU KNOWEST!
— F.B. MEYER

FROM HUMAN EYES 'TIS BETTER TO CONCEAL MUCH THAT I SUFFER, MUCH I HOURLY FEEL, BUT, OH, THIS THOUGHT CAN TRANQUILLIZE AND HEAL... ALL, ALL IS KNOWN TO THEE.

NAY... ALL BY THEE IS ORDERED, CHOSEN, PLANNED, EACH DROP THAT FILLS MY DAILY CUP, THY HAND PRESCRIBES FOR ILLS, NONE ELSE CAN UNDERSTAND, ALL, ALL IS KNOWN TO THEE!

— CHARLOTTE ELLIOTT

PSALM 143

THEREFORE IS MY SPIRIT OVERWHELMED WITHIN ME;
MY HEART WITHIN ME IS DESOLATE.

HEAR ME SPEEDILY, O LORD; MY SPIRIT FAILETH,
HIDE NOT THY FACE FROM ME, LEST I BE LIKE UNTO THEM
THAT GO DOWN INTO THE PIT.   VS. 4 & 7

AND, BEHOLD, THERE AROSE A GREAT TEMPEST IN THE
SEA, INSOMUCH THAT THE BOAT WAS COVERED WITH THE
WAVES; BUT HE WAS ASLEEP.   MATTHEW 8:24

MOST OF US KNOW WHAT IT IS TO BE OVERWHELMED
IN HEART; EMPTIED AS WHEN A MAN WIPETH A DISH AND TURNETH
IT UPSIDE DOWN; SUBMERGED AND THROWN ON OUR BEAM ENDS
LIKE A VESSEL MASTERED BY THE STORM... DISAPPOINTMENTS
AND HEART-BREAKS WILL DO THIS WHEN BILLOW AFTER BILLOW
ROLLS OVER US, AND WE ARE LIKE A BROKEN SHELL HURLED TO
AND FRO BY THE SURF. BLESSED BE GOD, AT SUCH SEASONS WE
ARE NOT WITHOUT AN ALL SUFFICIENT SOLACE, OUR GOD IS THE
HARBOUR OF WEATHER - BEATEN SAILS, THE HOSPICE OF
FORLORN PILGRIMS. HIGHER THAN WE ARE IS HE, HIS MERCY
HIGHER THAN OUR SINS, HIS LOVE HIGHER THAN OUR
THOUGHTS, IT IS PITIFUL TO SEE MEN PUTTING THEIR
TRUST IN SOMETHING LOWER THAN THEMSELVES; BUT OUR
CONFIDENCE IS FIXED UPON AN EXCEEDING HIGH AND
GLORIOUS LORD. A ROCK HE IS SINCE HE CHANGES NOT,
AND A HIGH ROCK BECAUSE THE TEMPESTS WHICH
OVER WHELM US ROLL FAR BENEATH HIS FEET; HE
IS NOT DISTURBED BY THEM, BUT RULES THEM AT HIS
WILL. IF WE GET UNDER THE SHELTER OF HIS LOFTY
ROCK WE MAY DEFY THE HURRICANE!
— C.H. SPURGEON

WE ARE TROUBLED ON EVERY SIDE, YET
NOT DISTRESSED; WE ARE PERPLEXED,
BUT NOT IN DESPAIR; PERSECUTED,
BUT NOT FORSAKEN; CAST DOWN,
BUT NOT DESTROYED!
2 CORINTHIANS 4:8,9

MY

BLESSED BE THE LORD, MY STRENGTH, WHO TEACHETH MY HANDS TO WAR, AND MY FINGERS TO FIGHT; MY GOODNESS, AND MY FORTRESS; MY HIGH TOWER, AND MY DELIVERER; MY SHIELD, AND HE IN WHOM I TRUST, WHO SUBDUETH MY PEOPLE UNDER ME.   VV. 1,2

TO KNOW HIM IN ALL THE VARIOUS ASPECTS OF HIS CHARACTER, AS LOVING-KINDNESS, FORTRESS, SHIELD, AND CONQUEROR—JESUS CAN BE THE SUPPLY OF YOUR EVERY NEED; AND AS THE DAYS PASS, YOU WILL PROBABLY FIND YOURSELF PUT INTO SITUATIONS WHICH WILL FORCE YOU TO DISCOVER IN HIM SOME NEW ASPECT, SOME FRESH CHARACTERISTIC, SOMETHING THAT WOULD NEVER HAVE APPEARED TO VIEW, TILL THE AWFUL EXIGENCY HAD RISEN —THEN PUT OUT YOUR HAND AND SAY MY!
— F.B. MEYER

HOW OFT IN THE CONFLICT, WHEN PRESSED BY THE FOE, I HAVE FLED TO MY REFUGE AND BREATHED OUT MY WOE; HOW OFTEN WHEN TRIALS LIKE SEA BILLOWS ROLL, HAVE I HIDDEN IN THEE, O THOU ROCK OF MY SOUL. HIDING IN THEE, HIDING IN THEE, THOU BLESSED ROCK OF AGES, I'M HIDING IN THEE!

GOD

PSALM 144

PSALM 145

EVERY DAY WILL I BLESS THEE, AND I WILL PRAISE THY NAME FOREVER AND EVER! DAVID WAS DETERMINED NEVER TO LET A DAY GO BY WITHOUT DISCOVERING SOME WAY TO FREIGHT IT DOWN WITH PRAISE. WHAT A NOBLE AMBITION TO EMULATE — AND ALL BECAUSE DAVID WAS LOOKING FORWARD TO PRAISING GOD FOREVER AND EVER IN YONDER BRIGHT REGIONS OF JOY. HE WANTED TO BE IN PRACTICE. WHEN HE ARRIVED ON THE GOLDEN SANDS BEYOND THE SHINING RIVER, HE DID NOT WANT TO START OUT IN KINDERGARTEN OF PRAISE AND LEARN HOW IT IS DONE. HE WANTED TO GRADUATE FROM EARTH WITH HIGH HONORS IN THE SUBJECT OF PRAISE AND TAKE HIS PLACE AT ONCE WITH THE WORTHIES ON THE OTHER SHORE. — JOHN PHILLIPS

GREAT IS THE LORD, AND GREATLY TO BE PRAISED; AND HIS GREATNESS IS UNSEARCHABLE!   Y3

EVERY MOMENT OF OUR LIVES, WE BREATHE, STAND, OR MOVE IN THE TEMPLE OF THE MOST HIGH; FOR THE UNIVERSE IS HIS TEMPLE. WHEREVER WE GO THE TESTIMONY OF HIS POWER, THE IMPRESS OF HIS HAND ARE THERE.

EVERYWHERE WE HEAR THY NAME, O GOD! EVERYWHERE WE SEE THY LOVE! THE UNIVERSE IS TO US THE BURNING BUSH WHICH THE HEBREW LEADER SAW; GOD IS PRESENT IN IT, FOR IT BURNS WITH HIS GLORY, AND THE GROUND ON WHICH WE STAND IS ALWAYS HOLY. — Y. DILLON

PSALM 146

Hallelujah!

THE GOD WHO MADE BOTH EARTH
AND HEAVEN, THE SEAS AND EVERY-
THING IN THEM. HE IS THE GOD WHO
KEEPS HIS PROMISE, AND GIVES
JUSTICE TO THE POOR AND
OPPRESED, AND FOOD TO THE
HUNGRY. HE FREES THE
PRISONERS, AND OPENS THE
EYES OF THE BLIND; HE LIFTS
THE BURDENS FROM THOSE
BENT DOWN BENEATH
THEIR LOADS. FOR
THE LORD LOVES
GOOD MEN.

V.V. 6-8

JEHOVAH CONSOLES
THE BEREAVED, CHEERS
THE DEFEATED, SOLACES
THE DESPONDENT, COMFORTS
THE DESPAIRING. LET THOSE WHO
ARE BOWED TO THE GROUND APPEAL
TO HIM, AND HE WILL SPEEDILY UPRAISE
THEM.
JEHOVAH MAKES THE UPRIGHT
TO BE HIS FAVOURED ONES. LET
THOSE WHO ENJOY THE INESTIMABLE
PRIVILEGE OF HIS LOVE MAGNIFY
HIS NAME WITH ENTHUSIASTIC DELIGHT.
... LOVED ONES, YOU MUST NOT BE
ABSENT FROM THE CHOIR! YOU MUST
NEVER PAUSE FROM HIS PRAISE
WHOSE INFINITE LOVE HAS MADE
YOU WHAT YOU ARE! - CHS

Hallelujah!

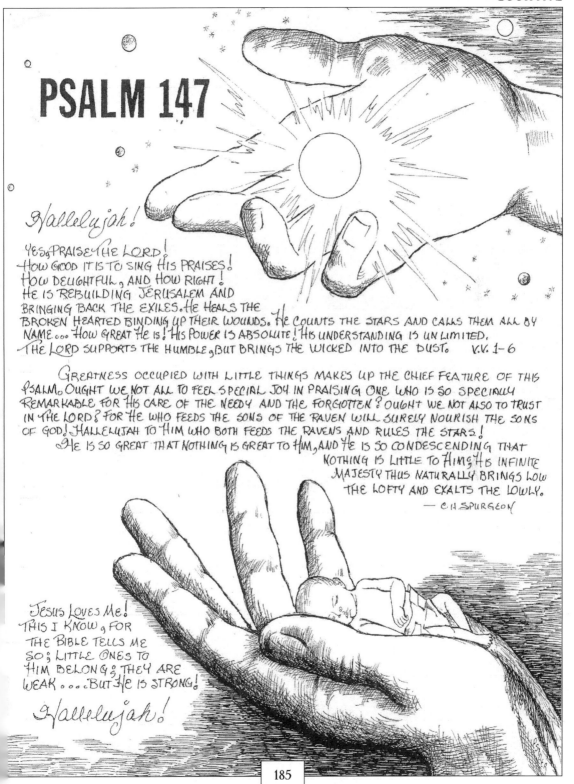

PSALM 147

Hallelujah!

YES, PRAISE THE LORD!
HOW GOOD IT IS TO SING HIS PRAISES!
HOW DELIGHTFUL, AND HOW RIGHT!
HE IS REBUILDING JERUSALEM AND
BRINGING BACK THE EXILES. HE HEALS THE
BROKEN HEARTED BINDING UP THEIR WOUNDS. HE COUNTS THE STARS AND CALLS THEM ALL BY
NAME... HOW GREAT HE IS! HIS POWER IS ABSOLUTE! HIS UNDERSTANDING IS UNLIMITED.
THE LORD SUPPORTS THE HUMBLE, BUT BRINGS THE WICKED INTO THE DUST.   V.V. 1-6

GREATNESS OCCUPIED WITH LITTLE THINGS MAKES UP THE CHIEF FEATURE OF THIS
PSALM. OUGHT WE NOT ALL TO FEEL SPECIAL JOY IN PRAISING ONE WHO IS SO SPECIALLY
REMARKABLE FOR HIS CARE OF THE NEEDY AND THE FORGOTTEN? OUGHT WE NOT ALSO TO TRUST
IN THE LORD? FOR HE WHO FEEDS THE SONS OF THE RAVEN WILL SURELY NOURISH THE SONS
OF GOD! HALLELUJAH TO HIM WHO BOTH FEEDS THE RAVENS AND RULES THE STARS!
HE IS SO GREAT THAT NOTHING IS GREAT TO HIM, AND HE IS SO CONDESCENDING THAT
NOTHING IS LITTLE TO HIM; HIS INFINITE
MAJESTY THUS NATURALLY BRINGS LOW
THE LOFTY AND EXALTS THE LOWLY.
— C.H. SPURGEON

JESUS LOVES ME!
THIS I KNOW, FOR
THE BIBLE TELLS ME
SO; LITTLE ONES TO
HIM BELONG; THEY ARE
WEAK....BUT HE IS STRONG!

Hallelujah!

PRAISE YE THE LORD. PRAISE YE THE LORD
FROM THE HEAVENS; PRAISE HIM IN THE
HEIGHTS.

PSALM 148

PRAISE HIM, ALL HIS ANGELS;
PRAISE YE HIM, ALL HIS HOSTS.
PRAISE YE HIM, SUN AND
MOON; PRAISE HIM
ALL YE STARS OF
LIGHT. PRAISE HIM,
YE HEAVENS. OF
HEAVENS, AND YE
WATERS THAT BE
ABOVE THE
HEAVENS. VV1-4

For unto us a child is born
unto us a Son is given
and the government shall be upon His shoulders

MESSIAH

and His name shall be called
Wonderful, Counsellor, the mighty God
the everlasting Father,
the Prince of Peace.

Isaiah 9:6

Praise Ye The Lord!

PSALM 149

Praise ye the Lord, the Al-might-y, the King of cre-a-

praise Him, for He is thy health and sal-va

PRAISE YE THE LORD
SING UNTO THE LORD A NEW SONG,
AND HIS PRAISE IN THE CONGREGATION
OF SAINTS.   V I.

THE PSALTER BEGINS WITH "BLESSED", AND ENDS WITH
"HALLELUJAH"! OBEDIENCE IN WALK AND CONDUCT LEADS TO
BLESSEDNESS, AND THIS CULMINATES IN RAPTURE. THE HEART THAT DOES
GODS WILL IN THIS WORLD MAY NOT BE ALWAYS HAPPY, BUT IT IS ALWAYS
BLESSED.... YOUR LIFE MAY RESEMBLE THE PSALTER WITH ITS VARYING
MOODS, ITS LIGHT AND SHADOW, ITS SOB AND SMILE; BUT IT WILL END WITH
HALLELUJAHS, IF ONLY YOU WILL KEEP TRUE TO THE WILL AND WAY AND WORK
OF THE MOST HOLY.

YOUR ESTIMATE OF THE WORLD IS OFTEN PESSIMISTIC TO THE LAST POINT; BUT
IF YOU WILL BE STILL, AND LET GOD FINISH HIS WORK PERFECTLY, YOU WILL HEAR ALL
THINGS THAT HAVE BREATH JOINING IN THE HALLELUJAH CHORUS, AND
SAYING, THE KINGDOMS OF THE WORLD HAVE BECOME THOSE OF
THE LORD AND OF HIS CHRIST!
GOD IS PREPARING THE WHOLE UNIVERSE
TO BE AN ORCHESTRA OF PRAISE AND ADORATION
TO HIS SON!

F. B. MEYER

Psalm 150

Hallelujah!

PRAISE HIM FOR HIS MIGHTY ACTS: PRAISE HIM ACCORDING TO HIS EXCELLENT GREATNESS

LET EVERYTHING THAT HATH BREATH PRAISE THE LORD

PRAISE YE THE LORD

JESUS

And he said unto them, These are the words which I spake unto you, while I was yet with you, that all things must be fulfilled, which were written in the law of Moses, and in the prophets, and in the psalms, concerning me.
Luke 24:44

Endnotes

Book I: Psalm 1-41

Psalm 1
The Living Bible, (Wheaton, Illinois: Tyndale House Publishers, 1971), Ps. 1:1-2 .

The King James Version in the New Scofield Reference Bible, (New York: Oxford University Press, 1967), Matt. 7:13-14.

Psalm 2
The Amplified Bible, (Grand Rapids, Michigan: Zondervan, 1987), Psalm 2: 9-11.

C.H. Spurgeon, *The Treasury of David,* vol 1, (McLean, Virginia: MacDonald Publishing Company), 12.

Psalm 3
King James Version, Psalm 3: 2-5.

C.H. Spurgeon, *The Treasury of David,* vol 1, (McLean, Virginia: MacDonald Publishing Company), 23.

Psalm 4
King James Version, Psalm 4:3, 4.

Psalm 5
King James Version, Psalm 5:3.

The Writings of Harriet Beecher Stowe, (Columbia University: Houghton, Mifflin and Co., 1896), 356.

Psalm 6
King James Version, Psalm 6: 8-9.

The Baptist Hymnal, Song, What a Friend We Have in Jesus, Joseph Scriven, (Nashville, Tennessee: Convention Press, 1991), 182._

Psalm 7
King James Version, Psalm 7:1, 2, 10; 1 Peter 5: 8-9.

Psalm 8
King James Version, Psalm 8:1, 3-5, 9.

Psalm 9
King James Version, Psalm 9:1-2.

Mrs. Charles Cowman. J. C McCauley quoted in *Streams in the Desert* Vol. 2 (Grand Rapids, Michigan: Zondervan, 1966), 95.

Psalm 10
King James Version, Psalm 10: 2, 12; I Peter 5:8.

F. B. Meyer, *Tried by Fire* (Fort Washington, Pennsylvania: Christian Literature Crusade), 183.

Psalm II
King James Version, Psalm 11:4.

C.H. Spurgeon, *The Treasury of David,* vol 1, (McLean, Virginia: MacDonald Publishing Company), 130.

Psalm 12
King James Version, Psalm 12:1-2.

C.H. Spurgeon, *The Treasury of David,* vol 1, (McLean, Virginia: MacDonald Publishing Company), 141-143.

Psalm 13
King James Version, Psalm 13:5, 6.

C.H. Spurgeon, *The Treasury of David,* vol 1, (McLean, Virginia: MacDonald Publishing Company), 153.

Psalm 14
King James Version, Psalm 14:7; Isaiah 64:1.

C.H. Spurgeon, *The Treasury of David,* vol 1, (McLean, Virginia: MacDonald Publishing Company), 164.

Psalm 15
King James Version, Psalm 15:1

F. B. Meyer, *Our Daily Homily,* (Westwood, New Jersey: Fleming H. Revel Co., 1966), 198.

Psalm 16
King James Version, Psalm 16:9-11.

F. B. Meyer, *Our Daily Homily,* (Westwood, New Jersey: Fleming H. Revel Co., 1966}, 198.

Psalm 17
King James Version, Psalm 17:1, 5; Isaiah 41:13.

The Baptist Hymnal, Song, "Precious Lord, Take My Hand", Thomas Dorsey, (Nashville, Tennessee: Convention Press, 1991), 456._

Psalm 18
King James Version, Psalm 18:1, 16, 17.

Psalm 19
King James Version, Psalm 19:1, 7.

C.H. Spurgeon, *The Treasury of David,* vol 1, (McLean, Virginia: MacDonald Publishing Company), 269-270.

Psalm 20
The Amplified Bible, Psalm 20:5.

C.H. Spurgeon, *The Treasury of David,* vol 1, (McLean, Virginia: MacDonald Publishing Company), 302.

Psalm 21
King James Version, Psalm 21:1-3; Hebrews 1:8-10.

Psalm 22
King James Version, Psalm 22:1; Mark 15:34.

Ray Overholt, song "He Could Have Called Ten Thousand Angels," 1958.

Psalm 23
King James Version, Psalm 23:1.

Elizabeth Clephane, song "The Ninety and Nine," 1868.

Psalm 24
King James Version, Psalm 24:9 -10.

F. B. Meyer, *Our Daily Homily,* (Westwood, New Jersey: Fleming H. Revel Co., 1966), 201.

Psalm 25
King James Version, Psalm 25:4-7.

The Baptist Hymnal, "He Leadeth Me O Blessed Thought", Joseph Gilmore, (Nashville, Tennessee: Convention Press, 1991), 52._

The Baptist Hymnal, Song, "Precious Lord, Take My Hand", Thomas Dorsey, (Nashville, Tennessee: Convention Press, 1991), 456._

Psalm 26
King James Version, Psalm 26:11-12.

Psalm 27
C.H. Spurgeon, *The Treasury of David,* Volume 1, (McLean, Virginia: MacDonald Publishing Company), 419. King James Version, Psalm 27:1, 4, 5; Romans 8:15.

Psalm 28
King James Version, Psalm 28:6-9.

F. B. Meyer, Our Daily Homily, (Westwood, New Jersey: Fleming H. Revel Co., 1966), 203.

C.H. Spurgeon, *The Treasury of David,* Volume 1, (McLean, Virginia: MacDonald Publishing Company), 23.

Psalm 29
King James Version, Psalm 29:1, 3, 4, 5, 7, 9.

F. B. Meyer, *Our Daily Homily,* (Westwood, New Jersey: Fleming H. Revel Co., 1966), 203.

Psalm 30
King James Version, Psalm 30:5.

F. B. Meyer, *Our Daily Homily,* (Westwood, New Jersey: Fleming H. Revel Co., 1966), 204.

Psalm 31
The Living Bible, Psalm 31:2-6.

Arthur Pink, *The Attributes of God,* (Grand Rapids, Michigan: Baker Book House, 1991), 51.

Psalm 32
King James Version, Psalm 32:7, 9, 11.

John Phillips, *Exploring the Psalms,* vol 1, (Neptune, New Jersey: Loizeaux Brothers, 1988), 244.

Psalm 33
King James Version, Psalm 33:1-5, 20.

John Phillips, *Exploring the Psalms,* vol 1, (Neptune, New Jersey: Loizeaux Brothers, 1988), 244.

Psalm 34
King James Version, Psalm 34:7.

John Phillips, *Exploring the Psalms,* vol 1, (Neptune, New Jersey: Loizeaux Brothers, 1988), 257.

Psalm 35
King James Version, Psalm 35:1-3, 9; Psalm 5:11.

C.H. Spurgeon, *The Treasury of David,* vol 1, (McLean, Virginia: MacDonald Publishing Company), 145.

Psalm 36
King James Version, Psalm 36:7.

C.H. Spurgeon, *The Treasury of David,* vol 1, (McLean, Virginia: MacDonald Publishing Company).

Psalm 37
King James Version, Psalm 37: 9-10, 39-40; Revelations 10:5-7.

Psalm 38
The Amplified Bible, Psalm 38:4, 13-15, 21-22; Romans 8:37.

C.H. Spurgeon, *The Treasury of David,* vol 1, (McLean, Virginia : MacDonald Publishing Company), 201.

Psalm 39
King James Version, Psalm 39:4-5.

C.H. Spurgeon, poem quoted from Sir John Davies in *The Treasury of David,* vol 1, (McLean, Virginia: MacDonald Publishing Company), 227.

Psalm 40
The Amplified Bible. Psalm 40:2-3

The Baptist Hymnal, Song, "Love Lifted Me", James Rowe, (Nashville, Tennessee: Convention Press, 1991), 546. John Phillips, *Exploring the Psalms,* vol 1, (Neptune, New Jersey: Loizeaux Brothers, 1988), 306.

Psalm 41
King James Version, Psalm 41:4-5, 10-11. The *Living Bible,* 2 Corinthians 4:8-10.

C.H. Spurgeon, *The Treasury of David,* vol 1, (McLean, Virginia: MacDonald Publishing Company), 260. Youth for Christ Songbook, "Safe Am I," Mildred Dillon, (Chicago, Illinois : Youth Publications, Inc.}.

Book 2: Psalm 42-72

Psalm 42
King James Version, Psalm 42:5.

C.H. Spurgeon, *The Treasury of David,* vol 1, (McLean, Virginia: MacDonald Publishing Company), 272.

Psalm 43
King James Version, Psalm 43:3 -4.

Ray Steadman, *Psalms: Folk Songs of Faith,* (Grand Rapids, Michigan : Discovery House Publishers, 2006), 107, 109.

Psalm 44
F. B. Meyer, *Our Daily Homily,* (Westwood, New Jersey: Fleming H. Revel Co., 1966), 209. *The Amplified Bible,* Psalm 44:4.

Psalm 45
New International Version, Psalm 45:10-11, 13-14.

John Phillips, *Exploring the Psalms,* vol 2, (Neptune, New Jersey: Loizeaux Brothers, 1988), 44-45.

Psalm 46
King James Version, Psalm 46:1 -3.

C.H. Spurgeon, *The Treasury of David,* vol 1, (McLean, Virginia : MacDonald Publishing Company), 340.

Psalm 47
King James Version, Psalm 47:6-9 .

C.H. Spurgeon, *The Treasury of David,* vol 1, (McLean, Virginia: MacDonald Publishing Company), 354.

Psalm 48
King James Version, Psalm 48:1, 10, 14; Rev. 19:1.

The Baptist Hymnal, Song, "How Great Thou Art", Stuart Hine, (Nashville, Tennessee: Convention Press, 1991), 10._

C.H. Spurgeon, *The Treasury of David,* vol 1, (McLean, Virginia: MacDonald Publishing Company), 362.

Psalm 49
King James Version, Psalm 49:6-8, 15; Matthew 20:28; I Peter 1:18-19.

William Barclay, *The Gospel of Matthew: Chapters 1-10,* (Westminster: John Knox Press, 2001).

Psalm 50
King James Version, Psalm 50:14, 15, 23.

Ray Steadman, *Psalms: Folk Songs of Faith,* (Grand Rapids, Michigan: Discovery House Publishers , 2006), 134.

Psalm 51
King James Version, Psalm 51:1, 10, 12-13.

C.H. Spurgeon, *The Treasury of David,* vol 1, (McLean, Virginia: MacDonald Publishing Company), 405.

Psalm 52
King James Version, Psalm 52:1, 5, 8.

C.H. Spurgeon, *The Treasury of David,* vol 1, (Mc-Lean, Virginia: MacDonald Publishing Company), 427-428.

F. B. Meyer, *Our Daily Homily,* (Westwood, New Jersey: Fleming H. Revel Co ., 1966), 212.

Psalm 53
King James Version, Psalm 53:1-2.

C.H. Spurgeon, T. B. Brooks as quoted in *The Treasury of David,* vol 1, (McLean, Virginia : MacDonald Publish in g Company), 167 -168.

Psalm 54
King James Version, Psalm 54:1-2, 4, 7.

Psalm 55
King James Version, Psalm 55:6-7.

The Baptist Hymnal, Song, "When Peace Like a River," (Nashville, Tennessee: Convention Press, 1991), 410.

Psalm 56
King James Version, Psalm 56:8; Malachi 3:16; Revelation 7:17.

Psalm 57
King James Version, Psalm 57:1; 91:1-4.

C.H. Spurgeon,*The Treasury of David,* vol 1, (McLean, Virginia: MacDonald Publishing Company) , 275-276 .

Psalm 58
King James Version, Psalm 58:11; Isaiah 11:4, 6. .

C.H. Spurgeon, *The Treasury of David,* vol 2, (McLean, Virginia: MacDonald Publishing Company), 4.

Psalm 59
King James Version, Psalm 59:1, 16, 17.

C.H. Spurgeon,*The Treasury of David,* vol 2, (McLean, Virginia: MacDonald Publishing Company), 18. *Youth For Christ Songbook,* song," Safe Am I," (Chicago, Illinois : Youth Publications, Inc.)

Psalm 60
The Amplified Bible, Psalm 60:4-5, 11-12; Isaiah 59:19.

C.H. Spurgeon,*The Treasury of David,* vol 2, (McLean, Virginia: MacDonald Publishing Company), 28-29.

Psalm 61
King James Version, Psalm 61:1-3.

William Orcutt and Ira Sankey, song, " O Safe to the Rock," 1881.

Psalm 62
Amplified Bible, Psalm 62:5-7.

C.H. Spurgeon, *The Treasury of David,* vol 2, (McLean, Virginia : MacDonald Publishing Company), 48, 77.

Psalm 63
King James Version, Psalm 63:1, 5, 7-8.

C.H. Spurgeon, *The Treasury of David,* vol 2, (McLean, Virginia: MacDonald Publishing Company), 67.

Psalm 64
King James Version, Psalm 64:1-4, 7, 10.

F. B. Meyer, *Our Daily Homily,* (Westwood, New Jersey: Fleming H. Revel Co ., 1966), 217-217.

Psalm 65
King James Version, Psalm 65:4, 6.

C.H. Spurgeon, *The Treasury of David,* vol 2, (McLean , Virginia: MacDonald Publishing Company), 91.

Psalm 66
King James Version, Psalm 66:8-10.

C.H. Spurgeon, *The Treasury of David,* vol 2, (McLean, Virginia: MacDonald Publishing Company), 111.

F. B. Meyer, *Our Daily Homily,* (Westwood, New Jersey: Fleming H. Revel Co., 1966), 217-218.

Psalm 67
King James Version, Psalm 67:1 -4, 7.

C.H. Spurgeon, *The Treasury of David,* vol 2, (McLean, Virginia: MacDonald Publishing Company), 129-130.

Psalm 68
The Amplified Bible, Psalm 68:7-8, 19, 35.

F. B. Meyer, *Our Daily Homily,* (Westwood, New Jersey: Fleming H. Revel Co., 1966), 218-219.

Psalm 69
The Amplified Bible, Psalm 69:20, 23; Isaiah 53:5.

The Baptist Hymnal, Song, "Man of Sorrow What

a Name", Phillip Bliss, (Nashville, Tennessee: Convention Press, 1991), 175.

Psalm 70
King James Version, Deuteronomy 32:11; Psalm 70:1, 4.

John Phillips, *Exploring the Psalms,* vol 2, (Neptune, New Jersey: Loizeaux Brothers, 1988), 262.

F. B. Meyer, *Our Daily Homily,* (Westwood, New Jersey: Fleming H. Revel Co., 1966),.

Psalm 71
King James Version, Psalm 71:1-3, 8.

C.H. Spurgeon, *The Treasury of David,* vol 2, (McLean, Virginia: MacDonald Publishing Company), 207-208.

Psalm 72
King James Version, Psalm 72:18-19.

Book 3: Chapters 73-89

Psalm 73
King James Version, Psalm 73:1-3, 17-18a, 28.

C.H. Spurgeon, *The Treasury of David,* vol 2, (McLean, Virginia: MacDonald Publishing Company), 253.

Psalm 74
King James Version, Psalm 74:18-20, 22.

F. B. Meyer, *Our Daily Homily,* (West wood, New Jersey: Fleming H. Revel Co ., 1966), 221.

Psalm 75
King James Version, Psalm 75: 7-9; John 10:27-28.

Psalm 76
King James Version, Psalm 76:1-3, 10. Quoted passage source unknown.

Psalm 77
King James Version, Psalm 77:1, 3, 11, 16.

Psalm 78
King James Version, Psalm 78:10-20, 40-41.

F. B. Meyer, *Our Daily Homily,* (Westwood, New Jersey: Fleming H. Revel Co., 1966), 222.

Psalm 79
The New Living Translation, (Wheaton, Illinois: Tyndale House Publishers, 1996), Psalm 79: 9, 13.

Mrs. Charles E. Cowman, *Streams in the Desert,* vol 1, (Grand Rapids, Michigan: Zondervan Publishing House, 1965), 61.

Psalm 80
King James Version, Psalm 80:14-15, 19; Isaiah 11:1-2.

Psalm 81
King James Version, Psalm 81:1, 10.

C.H. Spurgeon, *The Treasury of David,* vol 2, (McLean, Virginia: MacDonald Publishing Company), 402,405.

Psalm 82
King James Version, Psalm 82:8. Esther Walker, poem.

Psalm 83
King James Version, Psalm 83, 1-3, 13-15, 18.

The Baptist Hymnal, Song, "Like a River Glorious," Frances R. Havergale, (Nashville, Tennessee: Convention Press, 1991), 58.

Psalm 84
King James Version, Psalm 84:1 -4, 12.

John Phillips, *Exploring the Psalms,* (Neptune , New Jersey: Loizeaux Brothers, 1988), 94-95 .

Psalm 85
Psalm 85:1, 2, 7, 9.

Psalm 86
King James Version, Psalm 86:5, 10, 13, 15; Ephesians 3:20-21.

Psalm 87
King James Version, Psalm 87:3 ; Revelations 21:27.

The Baptist Hymnal, Song, "Glorious Things of Thee are Spoken," John Newton , (Nashville, Tennessee: Convention Press, 1991), 398 .

Psalm 88
King James Version, Psalm 88:1 -3, 6-7.

Youth For Christ Songbook, song," Jesus, Savior, Pilot me," (Chicago, Illinois: Youth Publications, Inc.), 108.

Psalm 89
King James Version, Psalm 89:1-4, 27, 29; Isaiah 9:6.

Book 4: Chapters 90-106

Psalm 90
King James Version, Psalm 90:1-2, 12.

The Baptist Hymnal, Song, " O God Our Help in Ages Past," Isaac Watt s, (Nashville, Tennessee: Convention Press , 1991), 74.

Psalm 91
King James Version, Psalm 91: 1-2, 4-5.

Psalm 92
King James Version, Psalm 92:1-2, 4-5, 12-15; 2 Cor. 4:1 6.

J. M . Boice, *Psalms,* vol. 2 (Grand Rapids, Michigan: Baker Books, 2005), 158.

Psalm 93
Ibid, Psalm 93:1, 4-5.

C.H. Spurgeon, *The Treasury of David,* vol 2, (McLean, Virginia: MacDonald Publishing Company), 134.

Psalm 94
King James Version, Psalm 94:1-2 . Esther Walker, Poem.

Psalm 95
King James Version, Psalms 95:1-5.

John Phillips, *Exploring the Psalms,* vol 3, (Neptune, New Jersey: Loizeaux Brothers, 1988), 193.

Psalm 96
New Living Translation, Psalm 96:1-3, 12-13.

The Baptist Hymnal, Song, "There' s Within My Heart a Melody," Luther Bridges, (Nashville, Tennessee: Convention Press, 1991), 435.

Psalm 97
King James Version, Psalm 97:1-5 .

C.H. Spurgeon, *The Treasury of David,* vol 2, (McLean, Virginia : MacDonald Publishing Company), 195.

Psalm 98
King James Version, Psalm 98 :1, 7-9.

F. B. Meyer, *Our Daily Homily,* (Westwood, New Jersey: Fleming H. Revel Co., 1966), 228 .

Psalm 99
King James Version, Psalm 99:1-3, 5; 1 Peter 1:15-16. *New International Version,* Isaiah 6:3; Rev. 4:8.

Psalm 100
King James Version, Psalm 100:4-5.

Psalm 101
*King James Version,*Psalm 101:1-3.

F. B. Meyer, *Our Daily Homily,* (Westwood, New Jersey: Fleming H. Revel Co., 1966) , 123 .

Psalm 102
King James Version, Psalm 102:12, 27.

F. B. Meyer, *Our Daily Homily,* (Westwood, New Jersey: Fleming H. Revel Co ., 1966), 231.

Psalm 103
King James Version, Psalm 103:1-5.

C.H. Spurgeon, *The Treasury of David,* vol 2, (McLean, Virginia: MacDonald Publishing Company), 277.

The Baptist Hymnal, Song, "Blessed Be the Name" Charles Wesley, (Nashville, Tennessee: Convention Press, 1991), 206.

Psalm 104
King James Version, Psalm 104:1-2, 19, 20.

Psalm 105
King James Version, Psalm 105 :39-43.

Psalm 106
King James Version, Psalm 106:1-3, 13-15.

F. B. Meyer, *Our Daily Homily,* (Westwood, New Jersey: Fleming H. Revel Co., 1966), 233.

Book 5: Chapters 107-150

Psalm 107
King James Version, Psalm 107:27-29.

Antoinette Wilson, poem "Wit's End Corner", (The Hulbert Publishing Co. Ltd., 1930).

Psalm 108
King James Version, Psalm 108:1, 4.

Youth for Christ Songbook, song," We Have an Anchor," Priscilla J. Owens (Chicago, Illinois: Youth Publications, Inc.), 381.

Psalm 109
King James Version, Psalm108:13; 109:1, 4, 21-22, 30-31.

F. B. Meyer, *Our Daily Homily,* (Westwood, New Jersey: Fleming H. Revel Co., 1966), 233.

Psalm 110
King James Version, Psalm 110:1 -2.

Psalm 111
King James Version, Psalm 111:1-4, 9.

Psalm 112
King James Version, Psalm 112:1-2, 6-8; Matthew 7:24-26.

F. B. Meyer, *Our Daily Homily,* (Westwood, New Jersey: Fleming H. Revel Co., 1966), 235.

Psalm 113
King James Version, Psalm 113:1-3.

John Phillips, *Exploring the Psalms,* vol 2, (Neptune, New Jersey: Loizeaux Brothers, 1988), 66.

Psalm 114
King James Version, Psalm 114:4, 7.

C.H. Spurgeon, *The Treasury of David,* vol 3, (McLean, Virginia: MacDonald Publishing Company), 43.

Psalm 115
The Living Bible, Psalm 115: 11-14.

C.H. Spurgeon, *The Treasury of David,* vol 3, (McLean, Virginia: MacDonald Publishing Company), 55.

Psalm 116
King James Version, Psalm 116:1-6.

C.H. Spurgeon, *The Treasury of David,* vol 3, (McLean, Virginia: MacDonald Publishing Company), 68.

Psalm 117
King James Version, Psalm 117:1-2.

C.H. Spurgeon, *The Treasury of David,* vol 3, (McLean, Virginia: MacDonald Publishing Company), 97.

F. M . Lehman, 'The Love of God", song in Favorites Volume 2, (Grand Rapids, Michigan: Zondervan Publishing House), 27.

Psalm 118
King James Version, Psalm 118:27; Romans 12:1; 2 Corinthians 5:14.

C.H. Spurgeon, *The Treasury of David,* vol 3, (McLean, Virginia: MacDonald Publishing Company), 113.

Psalm 119
Footnote Psalm 119 from *King James Version* in Scofield Reference Bible; Psalm 1-2. Verses 1-8

King James Version, Psalm 119:1, 3, 5. Habakkuk 3:6.

John Phillips, *Exploring the Psalms,* vol 2, (Neptune, New Jersey: Loizeaux Brothers, 1988), 108-109. Verses 9-16

King James Version, Psalm 119:9.

C.H. Spurgeon, *The Treasury of David,* vol 3, (McLean, Virginia: MacDonald Publishing Company), 157. Verses 17 -24

King James Version, Psalm 119:15-17, 24; Isaiah 58:11.

Ibid., Psalm 119:17-18.

Verses 25-32

King James Version, Psalm 119:25, 28.

C.H. Spurgeon, *The Treasury of David,* vol 3, (McLean, Virginia: MacDonald Publishing Company), 189, 191. Verses 33-40

King James Version, Psalm 119:33-35.

C.H. Spurgeon, *The Treasury of David,* vol 3, (McLean, Virginia: MacDonald Publishing Company), 209. Verses 41-48

King James Version, Psalm 119:44-48, 165.

C.H. Spurgeon, *The Treasury of David,* vol 3, (McLean, Virginia: MacDonald Publishing Company), 230. Verses 49-56

King James Version, Psalm 119:53-55.

C.H. Spurgeon, *The Treasury of David,* vol 3, (McLean, Virginia: MacDonald Publishing Company), 240, 242. Verses 57-64

King James Version, Psalm 119:57-60; Psalm 73:25-26, 28.

C.H. Spurgeon, *The Treasury of David,* vol 3, (McLean, Virginia: MacDonald Publishing Company), 260. Verses 65-72

King James Version, Psalm 119 :67, 68, 71: Luke 15:14-16.

C.H. Spurgeon, *The Treasury of David,* vol 3, (McLean, Virginia: MacDonald Publishing Company), 271, 273. Verses 73-80

King James Version, Psalm 119:73; Jeremiah 18:4.

F. B. Meyer, *Our Daily Homily,* (Westwood, New Jersey: Fleming H. Revel Co., 1966), 300-301. Verses 81-88

King James Version, Psalm 119:81-82.

C.H. Spurgeon, *The Treasury of David,* vol 3, (McLean, Virginia: MacDonald Publishing Company), 305. Verses 89-96

King James Version, Psalm 119:89-92.

C.H. Spurgeon, *The Treasury of David,* vol 3, (McLean, Virginia: MacDonald Publishing Company), 315. Verses 97-104

King James Version, Psalm 119:103; Exodus 16:31; Psalm 23:5; John 6:48-50.

C.H. Spurgeon, *The Treasury of David,* vol 3, (McLean, Virginia: MacDonald Publishing Company), 332. Verses 105-112

King James Version, Psalm 119:105, 110.

Verses 113-120

King James Version, Psalm 119:114-117.

C.H. Spurgeon, *The Treasury of David,* vol 3, (McLean, Virginia: MacDonald Publishing Company), 271, 355. *Youth For Christ Songbook,* song," Safe am I," Mildred Dillon, (Chicago, Illinois: Youth Publications, Inc.), 13. *The Baptist Hymnal,* Song, "Breath on Me," Edwin Hatch, (Nashville, Tennessee: Convention Press, 1991), 238. Verses 121-128

King James Version, Psalm 119:126 -127.

C.H. Spurgeon, *The Treasury of David,* vol 3, (McLean, Virginia: MacDonald Publishing Company), 370. Verses 129-136

King James Version, Psalm 119:129, 130, 133, 135.

C.H. Spurgeon, *The Treasury of David,* vol 3, (McLean, Virginia: MacDonald Publishing Company), 378. Verses 137-144

King James Version, Psalm 119:140-141, 144; Psalm 107; John 7:37.

Verses 145-152

King James Version, Psalm 119:145, 147, 148, 151.

C.H. Spurgeon, *The Treasury of David,* vol 3, quotes by Thomas Brooks and John Morrison, (McLean, Virginia: MacDonald Publishing Company}, 271,405, 407.

Verses 153 -160

King James Version, Psalm 119:159.

The Baptist Hymnal, Song, "Breathe on Me Breath of God," Edwin Hatch, (Nashville, Tennessee: Convention Press, 1991), 238.

Verses 161 -168

The Living Bible, Psalm 119:162, 163, 167, 168.

C.H. Spurgeon, *The Treasury of David,* vol 3, (McLean, Virginia : MacDonald Publishing Company}, 423. Verses 169-176

King James Version, Psalm 119:169, 176; 1 Peter 2:25.

L. Phillip Knox, song, "The One Lost Sheep," copyright 1977.

Psalm 120
King James Version, Psalm 120:1.

C.H. Spurgeon, *The Treasury of David,* vol 3, (McLean, Virginia: MacDonald Publishing Company}, 5-6.

Psalm 121
King James Version, Psalm 121:4-6.

Dr. Herbert Lockyer, *All the Promises of the Bible,* (Grand Rapids, Michigan: Zondervan Publishing House, 1962), 130.

Psalm 122
King James Version, Psalm 122:6-7.

F. B. Meyer, *Our Daily Homily,* (Westwood, New Jersey: Fleming H. Revel Co., 1966}, 239.

Psalm 123
King James Version, Psalm 123:1 -2.

F. B. Meyer, *Our Daily Homily,* (Westwood, New Jersey: Fleming H. Revel Co., 1966}, 239. Stuart Hamblen, Song, "Until Then," (Hamblen Music Company, 1958}.

Psalm 124
King James Version, Psalm 124:7-8.

The Baptist Hymnal, Song, "O for a Thousand Tongues to Sing," Charles Wesley (Nashville, Tennessee: Convention Press, 1956}, 216.

C.H. Spurgeon, *The Treasury of David,* vol 3, (McLean, Virginia: MacDonald Publishing Company}, 51.

Psalm 125
King James Version, Psalm 125:2; Zechariah 25.

F. B. Meyer, *Our Daily Homily,* (Westwood, New Jersey: Fleming H. Revel Co., 1966), 240.

Psalm 126
King James Version, Psalm 126:5 -6.

F. B. Meyer, *Our Daily Homily,* (Westwood, New Jersey: Fleming H. Revel Co., 1966), 240.

Psalm 127
King James Version, Psalm 127:3-5.

John Phillips, *Exploring the Psalms,* vol 5, (Neptune, New Jersey: Loizeaux Brothers, 1988), 68.

Psalm 128
King James Version, Psalm 128:1-4.

Psalm 129
King James Version, Psalm 129:1-2; 2 Corinthians 4:17.

F. B. Meyer, *Our Daily Homily,* (Westwood, New Jersey: Fleming H. Revel Co., 1966}, 241.

Psalm 130
King James Version, Psalm 130:1.

Psalm 131
King James Version, Psalm 131:1, 2.

George Croly, "Spirit of God , Descend Upon My Heart, " (Public Domain: 1854).

Psalm 132
King James Version, Psalm 132:13-16; 1 Corinthians 3:16.

Psalm 133
King James Version, Psalm 133:1-3; 1 John 4:11.

F. B. Meyer, *Our Daily Homily,* (Westwood, New Jersey: Fleming H. Revel Co., 1966), 243.

Psalm 134
King James Version, Psalm 134:1-2, Psalm 34:1.

F. B. Meyer, *Our Daily Homily,* (Westwood, New Jersey: Fleming H. Revel Co., 1966), 243.

Psalm 135
King James Version, Psalm 135:1.

C.H. Spurgeon, *The Treasury of David,.*vol 3, (McLean, Virginia: MacDonald Publishing Company), 183.

Psalm 136
King James Version, Psalm 136:1.

The Baptist Hymnal, Song, "There's a Wideness in God's Mercy," D. Wagner, (Nashville, Tennessee : Convention Press, 1 991), 25.

Psalm 137
Living Bible, Psalm 137:1-2.

F. B. Meyer, *Our Daily Homily,* (Westwood, New Jersey: Fleming H. Revel Co., 1966), 244.

Psalm 138
King James Version, Psalm 23:4; Psalm 138:1, 6-7.

Psalm 139
King James Version, Psalm 139 :1, 5, 9-10, 23-24.

The Baptist Hymnal, Song, " He Leadeth Me," Joseph Gilmore, (Nashville , Tennessee: Convention Press, 1 991), 52.

Psalm 140
King James Version, Psalm 140:1, 7; Luke 10:3.

F. B. Meyer, Our Daily Homily, (Westwood, New Jersey: Fleming H. Revel Co., 1966), 246.

Psalm 141
King James Version, Psalm 141:2 -3; James 3:2.

C.H. Spurgeon, *The Treasury of David*, vol 3, (McLean, Virginia : MacDonald Publishing Company), 308, 315.

Psalm 142
King James Version, Psalm 142:3, 7.

F. B. M eyer, *Our Daily Homily,* (Westwood, New Jersey: Fleming H. Revel Co., 1966), 246-247.

C.H. Spurgeon, Charlotte Elliot as quoted in *The Treasury of David,* vol 3, (McLean, Virginia: MacDonald Publishing Company), 328.

Psalm 143
King James Version, Psalm 143 :4, 7; Matthew 8:24; 2 Corinthians 4:8-9.

C.H. Spurgeon, William Nicholson as quoted in *The Treasury of David,* vol 3, (McLean, Virginia: MacDonald Publishing Company) .

Psalm 144
King James Version, Psalm 144:1-2.

F. B. M eyer, *Our Daily Homily* , (Westwood, New Jersey: Fleming H. Revel Co., 1966), 247.

Psalm 145
King James Version, Psalm 145 :2-3.

John Phillips, *Exploring the Psalms,* vol 1, (Neptune, New Jersey: Loizeaux Brothers , 1988), 240.

C.H. Spurgeon, *The Treasury of David,* vol 3, (McLean, Virginia: MacDonald Publishing Company), 389-390.

Psalm 146
King James Version, Psalm 146:5, 6, 8.

C.H. Spurgeon, *The Treasury of David,* vol 3, (McLean, Virginia: MacDonald Publishing Company), 403.

Psalm 147
Living Bible, Psalm 147 :1-6.

C.H. Spurgeon, *The Treasury of David,* vol 3, (McLean, Virginia: MacDonald Publishing Company), 417.

The Baptist Hymnal, Song, "Jesus Loves Me," Anna Warner, (Nashville, Tennessee: Convention Press, 1991), 344.

Psalm 148
King James Version, Psalm 148:1-4; Isaiah 9:6.

Psalm 149
King James Version, Psalm 149:1.

F. B. Meyer, *Our Daily Homily,* (Westwood, New Jersey: Fleming H. Revel Co., 1966), 249.

Joachim Neander (author-1680), "Praise Ye the Lord, the Almighty," (translated by Catherine Winkworth (1863), public domain).

Psalm 150
King James Version, Psalm 150:2, 6.